Visions for Oxford
in the 21st century

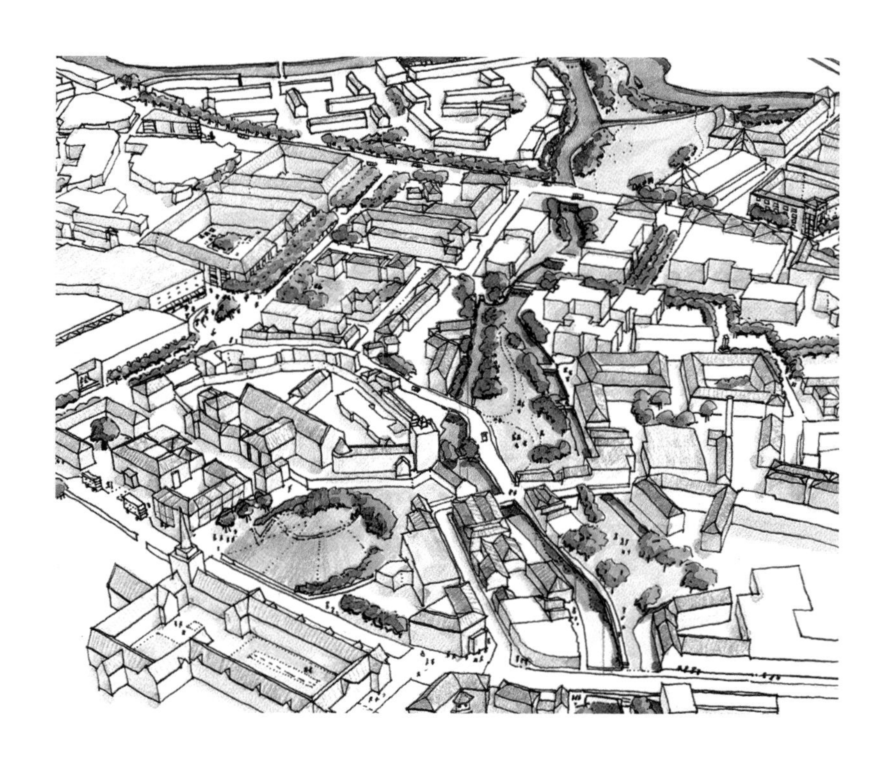

In memory of
Edwin Townsend-Coles
1922-2003

Chairman of Oxford Civic Society 1993-2000
tireless champion of a better Oxford

Published by
Oxford Civic Society, PO Box 149, Oxford OX2 7ZX

Copyright © 2003 Oxford Civic Society
First published 2003
ISBN 0-9501236-2-5

Editorial team:
Michael Havinden, Chair, Genefer Clark, Frank Dann, Tony Joyce,
Kate Miller, Edwin Townsend-Coles.

Views expressed by the contributors are their own, not those of Oxford Civic Society.

Acknowledgements:

Illustrations from the Urban Design Strategy
by Roger Evans Associates
courtesy of Oxford City Council

Designed by Colophon Media, Oxford
Printed by Oxfam Print Unit, Oxford

Contents

Part One: Visions for the City's Life

Part Two: Designing a Better City

Part Three: Forecasts

Part Four: The Last Word

Contributors

The Chairman and Committee of Oxford Civic Society wish to acknowledge with warm thanks the expertise, trouble and patience of our contributors.

Mark Barrington-Ward, a member of the Civic Society's Planning Sub-Committee, has known Oxford since 1948 when his family moved to the city and he came up to Balliol College to read History. From 1961-79, he was editor of the *Oxford Mail*, the evening paper for the Oxford area.

Christopher Brown has been Director of the Ashmolean Museum since 1998. He was at the National Gallery, London, from 1971 to 1998 and his area of expertise is Dutch and Flemish 17th century paintings. He is Chairman of the National Loan Collection Trust.

Emily Brown is an undergraduate student at Southampton University. She grew up in Oxford.

Martyn Brown is the Museums and Heritage Officer for Oxfordshire County Council and is based at the Oxfordshire Museum at Woodstock. He was formerly Director of Museums in Jersey and a freelance museums' consultant and author. He has lived in Woodstock since 1988.

Christine Burgess is Co-ordinator of the Oxford Confederation of Artists and Makers (OXCAM) which represents the many artists and craftspeople in Oxfordshire.

John Chipperfield is an assistant editor of the *Oxford Mail* and a sports enthusiast.

Maureen Christian is an Oxford City Councillor and a former Lord Mayor of Oxford. She is a past President of the National Association of British Markets Authorities and previously chaired Oxford City Council Planning Committee.

David Coleman is Professor of Demography at Oxford University. Between 1985-87 he worked for the Government as Special Adviser. He has published over 80 papers and 8 books on demography. In 1997 he was elected to the Council of the International Union for the Scientific Study of Population.

Debbie Dance is Secretary of Oxford Preservation Trust. A chartered surveyor with an MSc in Historic Conservation from Oxford Brookes University, she sits on the South East Panel of the Heritage Lottery Fund and is a national judge for the Royal Institution of Chartered Surveyors.

Mark Davies lives on a canal boat and has published several articles and books on Oxford's waterways.

Roger Evans is an architect, town planner and urban designer. He is a past Chair of the Urban Design Group and has advised the Department of the Environment, Transport and the Regions on design in the planning system. He has been responsible for preparing urban design frameworks for towns and cities throughout the UK and abroad.

Frideswide Middle School has become the junior section of the Cherwell School, Marston Ferry Road. Miss Thompson's class in Year 8 in 2002 were aged twelve and thirteen.

Edmund Gray is a former Inspector of Historic Buildings at the Department of the Environment and author of *The British House: a Concise Architectural History.* He first lived in Oxford in 1940-43 and since then has never been long absent.

Michael Havinden is Chair of the editorial committee of this book and is Vice-Chair of Oxford Civic Society. He was an Oxford postgraduate in the 1950s and a Senior Lecturer in Economic and Social History at the University of Exeter until 1995. He retired to live in Oxford in 1996.

Moyra Haynes is Chairman of the Oxford Consumers' Group and was Secretary of Oxford Preservation Trust 1990-8. She is a Deputy Lieutenant of Oxfordshire.

Rosalind Lacey has been Chair of Home-Start, Oxford since 1999. She was formerly employed as a senior manager in Adult Education, London Borough of Hillingdon. She is now a part-time tutor for Oxford University Department of Continuing Education and the WEA.

Paul Langford has been Professor of Modern History at Oxford University since 1996 and Rector of Lincoln College since 2000. He has been general editor of *The Oxford History of the British Isles* from 1996. He is Chairman of 'Oxford Inspires', the company which organised Oxford's bid to be European Capital of Culture in 2008.

Marcus Lapthorn has been General Manager of Expressway Oxford, the company which is planning to introduce guided transit buses to link north and south Oxford. He was formerly Oxford's City Centre Manager.

Sir Colin Lucas is the Vice-Chancellor of Oxford University and was Master of Balliol College 1994 to 2001. He was Professor of History at the University Of Chicago 1990-4.

Kate Miller, one of the editors of this book, is currently Planning Secretary of Oxford Civic Society. She has lived in Oxford since 1962.

Jeremy Mogford is the founder of Browns Restaurant on Woodstock Road. On Banbury Road, he owns Old Parsonage Hotel and Gee's Restaurant and on High Street, Old Bank Hotel, Quod Restaurant and Bar.

Anna Murray, herself a former therapist, is now a Clinical Trustee of the Oxford Parent Infant Project (OXPIP).

Charles Parrack is Senior Lecturer in Planning at Oxford Brookes University School of Architecture. With his students, he has been involved for some years in Mapping Matters, projects which encourage residents to create planning schemes.

John Preston is Reader in Transport Studies and Director of the Oxford University Transport Studies Unit, which is a research unit of the School of Geography and the Environment. He has extensive experience in transport research and has managed over 60 research grants and contracts.

Alan Russell, OBE, qualified in Economics and Politics at Oxford University and in Architectural History and Historical Conservation at Oxford Brookes/Oxford University Department of Continuing Education. He is a founder member and currently Chairman of the Dresden Trust.

Anthony Smith, CBE, has been President of Magdalen College since 1988. He was a BBC Current Affairs Producer and Director of the British Film Institute 1979-88. He is the author of *The Oxford Illustrated History of Television*, published in 1995. He became President of Oxford Civic Society in 2001.

Helen Lawton Smith is Reader in Local Economic Development in the Centre for Local Economic Development at Coventry University. She is the founder and Director of Research at the Oxfordshire Economic Observatory, an independent research centre based in the School of Geography and the Environment at Oxford University.

Cora Spencer has worked with the African Caribbean Action Network and the Oxford Racial Equality Council and as a voluntary adult education adviser.

Clare Symonds has co-operated with Charles Parrack and the Oxford Brookes University Planning Department in organising Mapping Matters projects. For some years she was the city council officer responsible for putting Agenda 21 sustainability schemes into practice in Oxford.

Lucy Tennyson is a freelance journalist and runs her own PR consultancy based in Oxford. She is interested in environmental and health issues and works on a regular basis for Oxford Brookes University, Age Concern and the RSPB.

Dick Thomas lives in Headington. He has been a member of the Civic Society since its early days. Amongst his published poems is an illustrated collection in aid of local charities.

Keith Thomson is currently Director of the Oxford University Museum. Amongst posts he held in the United States were Professor of Biology at Yale University, Director of the Peabody Museum of Natural History and Distinguished Scientist in Residence at the New School for Social Research in New York.

John Thompson runs Fletcher Thompson Associates, a Landscape Design Practice. He is the Co-ordinator of the Forest of Oxford scheme, which undertakes tree planting throughout the city, and was formerly Chief Landscape Architect of Oxford City Council

Edwin Townsend-Coles was Chairman of Oxford Civic Society from 1993 until 2000 and administered the Oxfordshire Blue Plaques scheme on behalf of the Society. He was formerly Director of Adult Education at the University of Rhodesia and Nyasaland, a UNESCO consultant and Adviser to the Permanent Secretary of the Ministry of Education in Botswana.

Michel Treisman is a Fellow of New College and Emeritus Reader in the Oxford University Department of Psychology.

Graham Upton has been Vice-Chancellor of Oxford Brookes University since 1997. At Birmingham University, he was Professor of Educational Psychology 1988-93 and Pro-Vice-Chancellor 1993-7.

Priscilla Waugh is a New Zealander who now lives in Oxford. Author of *Searching the Thames*, she has written for some broadsheets as well as magazines here and abroad; she currently contributes a monthly column about her wild garden to *The Oxford Times*.

Sir David Weatherall, FRS, is Emeritus Regius Professor of Medicine and Honorary Director of the Weatherall Institute of Molecular Medicine, Oxford University. His major research contributions, resulting in over 700 publications, have been in the field of clinical, biochemical and molecular medicine and in disease prevention throughout the world.

Sir Martin Wood OBE, FRS, DL, with his wife Audrey, founded Oxford Instruments, the first spin out from Oxford University, in 1959. The company makes equipment for research using high magnetic fields and cryogenics.

Mike Woodin is leader of the Green Group on Oxford City Council and a former principal speaker of the national Green Party. He is Lecturer in Psychology at Balliol College, Oxford.

Preface

By Anthony Smith

Fifty years ago on the first (and last) days of every term there would be piles of large wooden trunks covering platforms at Oxford station, the kind you can now pick up in antique shops; large trucks would cart them around the city depositing them at college lodges and at the houses of that no longer existing phalanx of landladies who took care of most of the student population. Today those scenes have their counterpart, on the days when hundreds of parental vehicles fill the streets around the colleges, dutifully proud parents carting computers, teddy bears, sports equipment, musical instruments and books in cardboard boxes. At the eastern end of the town once lived a completely different population, of automobile workers, skilled and unskilled, their foremen and managers. Today, furnished with two universities, Oxford populations are intermingled, the complex hierarchies of town and gown dissolving, partly under the influence of new high-tech industries; today the life chances of these mingled communities are no longer visibly defined by different levels of wealth, aspiration, education or nourishment, nor by the streets or quarters in which they reside.

The hardware of a city never catches up with the software of its forms of life. The demands which these ever-changing forms make on the physical structure of a city are impossible to calculate or predict. They are subject to shifting ideologies, legislative vagaries, conflicting perceptions of the future and the influences of global forces beyond any possibility of local influence. What can be done is to study them and describe them and set out ways in which the enduring character of a place can be helped to survive the great tides of changing taste and social need which strike it, decade by decade.

The essays that follow offer explanations and visions of Oxford that are proof of a continuing civic patriotism. In this century we have all grown to accept too easily that the built environment is subject more to remote economic forces than to people who inhabit it, but the reader will, I hope, come away from this book, as I have, feeling that there is much that we can do to maintain and enhance the life of this flourishing town, unique for its wealth of buildings and fine objects, enveloped in its history and mystique which seem to survive all official attempts to disillusion, its very name continuing to evoke, everywhere in the world, the sense of high standards which no reality can reach. Oxford is far from being one of its own legendary lost causes, though many good things have been lost. But its future is perhaps more in our control than we sometimes realise.

I found myself heartened and encouraged when I had read these papers. Oxford and its environs are rich in rivers, landscape, gardens, buildings as well as in the lives of learning and industry. All of these are in one way or another under constant threat and can be maintained only through the vigilance of the many people who care in a determined way for one aspect of the place or another – or all of them at once. The place is a magnet of loyalties which transcend the country in which it is situated, an academic version of a holy city perhaps. So it is excellent that in *Visions for Oxford* a collection of heterogeneous ideas have been brought together about where Oxford should be going, and how it might survive, and more than survive, the powerful disintegrating forces at work in our society.

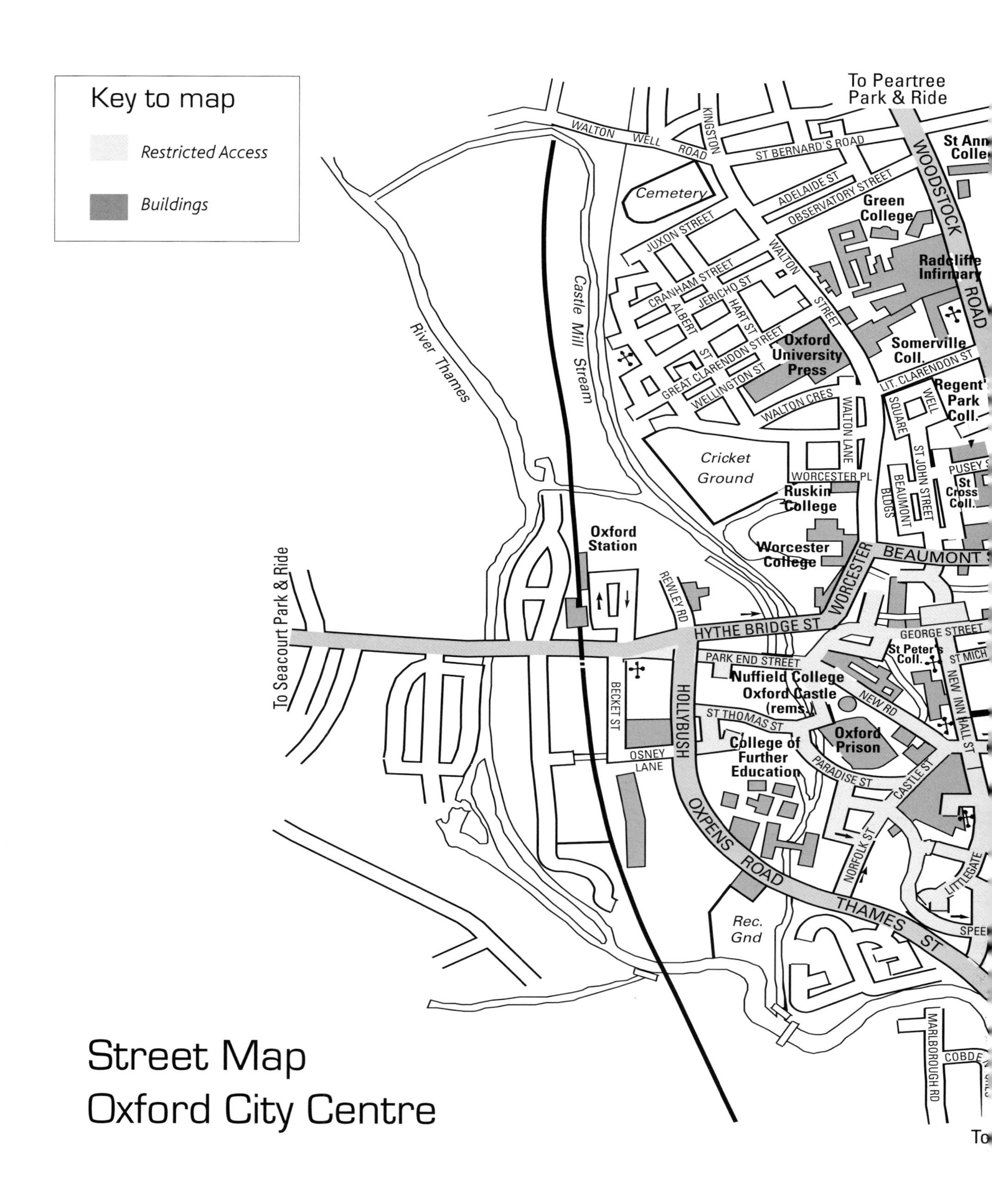

Street Map
Oxford City Centre

This shift to restraining traffic in the university area, which began in the 1970s when Radcliffe Square, New College Lane and Holywell were closed as through routes, and the success of the 1960s appeal to restore the historic buildings of the colleges and university, mean that these can now probably be seen to better advantage than for a generation.

Another achievement on the credit side has been the protection after an uncertain start of the views of Oxford's spires and towers and of the ancient city's green setting. After the city council had allowed the university's new engineering and biochemistry buildings to project slablike into the famous skyline, a proposal by the university to build a tower for zoology twice as high as the spire of St Mary's alerted the council to the dangers. The city council adopted a high buildings policy which allows small-scale additions like the ziggurat on the new Said Business School, but nothing else.

The protection of green views into, from and inside the city began before the Second World War when the Oxford Preservation Trust - the local mini-National Trust which recently celebrated its 75th anniversary - started to buy land in strategic places, making gifts to the city council of South Park and Shotover. The protection of the western side of Oxford, threatened by the spread of housing at Botley and up Cumnor Hill, was also increased during the war when, with the support of the Trust, the last private owner of the Wytham estate gave part and sold the rest on favourable terms to Oxford University on condition that the "great natural beauty" of the estate should be preserved. This pioneering effort was enormously strengthened by the official establishment in the 1950s of a green belt round the city, although the inner boundary remained interim until the 1990s because of disputes about where and how tightly it should be drawn. While the flood plain to some extent safeguarded the river valleys, the hills were at risk. The green belt has been a vital instrument in protecting the special character of Oxford by containing urban sprawl and establishing a defined edge between town and country.

On the debit side the disaster of post-war planning was the handling of St Ebbe's. Under a programme for comprehensive redevelopment, the people there were rehoused, largely against their wishes, in new council estates on the edge of the city. The biggest, Blackbird Leys, became an offshore island on the far side of the ring road - the size of a small town but for some time lacking any of a town's amenities, with a centre that became a jumble of unrelated buildings and with at one point a disproportionate number of the city's schoolchildren.

The story of St Ebbe's has been presented as the smashing up of a community at the behest of commercial interests anxious to expand. But it was more complicated than that. The council was not at first in favour of expanding shopping in the city centre, influenced by supporters of the twin city concept who thought that the way to save the historic city and reduce traffic congestion was to create a new shopping centre for the car workers and their families east of Magdalen Bridge, and possibly a new civic centre too. The council fought to prevent Woolworths from knocking down the historic Clarendon Hotel to build a new Cornmarket store, now part of the Clarendon Centre, as it wanted the store to be built instead at the proposed new shopping centre for Cowley. But the pass was sold when the Minister, Harold Macmillan, allowed an appeal by Woolworths. Marks and Spencer had to be allowed to rebuild in Cornmarket as well, and others followed. The city persevered with creating its Cowley shopping centre, including the city's first multi-storey car park, but it became clear that this could not become a substitute for the city centre shops.

The council's condemnatory attitude to St Ebbe's was conditioned by the fact that before the war, blighted by the gasworks, it had been declared a slum clearance area. Post-war euphoria about the possibilities of planning also played a part, encouraging the idea that St Ebbe's should be reshaped to provide space for additional civic needs using widened legal powers while people were given homes of a higher standard on new estates. It was typical of the time that Dr Thomas Sharp, who prepared the first post-war plan for the city including a pioneering and outstandingly sensitive analysis of its historic townscape, also proposed the most drastic demolitions. He labelled not only St Ebbe's and Jericho but also Victorian North Oxford as outworn, although he wanted to keep its trees!

The proposal, following the 1964 development plan, to build a modern, covered shopping centre in St Ebbe's seemed a constructive step after years of dereliction and delay. It included a new department store for which consumers had asked. It used the fall of the land to allow the shops to be serviced from underneath, avoiding the congestion apparent in Cornmarket and Queen Street, with a deck above giving a level buggy-push from Queen Street to a multi-storey car park. It also provided a badly needed larger public library. The disappearance of the job lot of buildings at the end of Queen Street, long known as MacFisheries Corner, seemed no loss.

The reality proved disillusioning. Westgate was too dominant and inward-looking. The street pattern was obliterated and some old houses destroyed needlessly, with only a handful getting a last-minute reprieve after the Preservation Trust stepped in. Partly because of the long uncertainty where relief roads might go, far from being comprehensively planned, development was piecemeal. Buildings like the College of Further Education and the Ice Rink look as if they have just been dropped down amid surface car parks.

But what tends to be forgotten is that St Ebbe's has also been the scene in the same period of one enormous improvement to the city - the removal of the gas works from both banks of the river and the redemption of Oxford's riverside. Dr Sharp, printing pictures of the stretch where the Thames flowed through the gasworks, commented that it might be the river of any northern industrial town. Today there is a park on part of the gasworks site and footpaths on both banks. The bridge which carried the gas pipes and rail wagons has become a decorative footbridge to the park. Another footbridge gives South Oxford a more direct route to the city centre.

The arts and crafts-inspired housing on the northern bank, built in the late 1970s to a master plan commissioned by the city council, compares favourably with any development since, not least the ponderous Edwardian pastiche now in vogue.

Councillors and officials also showed they could learn, if in some cases reluctantly, from their mistakes. Jericho escaped the fate of St Ebbe's. Rehabilitation became the watchword, although there were still some demolitions in Jericho, mainly for a new school. Before the war a committee of the Oxford Architectural and Historical Society had led the way in listing old houses in the city that ought to be preserved. A reaction nationally and locally in favour of making the most of the legacy from the past led to Victorian North Oxford becoming the first of what are now 16 conservation areas. The appointment of the city's first conservation officer in 1972 was a milestone.

A train crossing the gasworks bridge beside a gasholder c. 1925.
© Oxfordshire County Council Photographic Archive

When the city embarked on another major redevelopment of council-owned land in the 1980s at Gloucester Green, it abandoned after public consultation the idea of creating another large covered shopping mall and chose the "romantic option", incorporating shops, a bus station and a new site for the open air market above an underground car park. The eclectic post-modern architecture with its Disney touches looks rather like a stage set, but has proved popular. Unfortunately the otherwise welcome increase in the number of buses produced by government deregulation made the bus station inadequate from the start and it has no setting down space for passengers being delivered or met by taxi or car.

The city council's proposals in the 1990s for two large projects in partnerships led by developers have been less successful. Both were rightly criticised on design grounds. The plan for a leisure development next to the ice rink, aptly dubbed by its opponents Shed City, was rejected after a public inquiry.

A second proposal for a big extension of Westgate was said to be required to help meet the demand for shops in central Oxford; a demand that refutes any contention that the city centre is declining economically because of the councils' transport strategy. This unsatisfied demand has been blamed for the ever-increasing rents which have reduced the number of specialist local shops in the centre, although it seemed unlikely that the proposed extension would solve this problem since the most likely tenants of the new shops were national retailers. The scheme also included a bus hub which would have taken the bus stops out of Queen Street, allowing it to be completely pedestrianised, and a large underground car park to replace the existing multi-storey one which is badly in need of refurbishment.

But the proposed monolithic block broke the city's own height limits and was turned down by the Minister after a public inquiry on the ground that its scale and design would cause harm. He added that the city was thriving and questioned the appropriateness of so large a development "so close to the centre of this historic university city." The Minister in turn was told to reconsider after the terms of his decision letter were criticised by a High Court judge and a new scheme is now in preparation..

The future of the council-owned land in St Ebbe's still presents a great opportunity. This is all the greater now that the historic castle and prison site, owned by the county council, is being opened up following the closure of Oxford prison and that the railway station may be moved to the Oxpens area. There is a last chance to provide more public amenities. These could include a coach station more accessible by bus, car and taxi and linked to the railway station, with Gloucester Green perhaps becoming a setting down point for tourist coaches, and, if financially feasible, the large hall for conferences and concerts which has been talked about for over 50 years. If the Oxpens quarter and the castle and prison area can, through the provision of more through routes and improved urban design, be better knitted into the fabric of the city, some of the mistakes of the recent past will be rectified. But the architecture must be design and not developer led.

The underlying difficulty for the planners, which inevitably also affects the region of which Oxford is the centre, has been how to reconcile the policy of preserving the city's character by limiting its size and population, and putting a green belt round it, with demands for growth in the national interest, and to keep the city's economy prospering.

Just after the war this pressure came most conspicuously from the motor industry which demanded more houses for the workers needed if exports were to be expanded. Dr Sharp even suggested the industry should be moved away completely from Oxford to protect the historic city and reduce an unhealthy dependence on one source of employment, but this was rejected as impracticable.

The council instead, with the support of the Minister for Housing and Local Government, tried to limit the number employed at Cowley to around 16,000. It also adopted a policy, which has been the bedrock of planning ever since, of not allowing any large new employer into the city and of limiting expansion to small firms and to businesses that were already established or had a special need to be in Oxford.

But, although Pressed Steel was persuaded to build a new body plant in Swindon, the number of workers at Cowley rose to a peak of around 28,000. It then fell to under a fifth of that figure with the sad and largely self-inflicted collapse of the British-owned motor industry and the closure of the old Morris works. The happier ending is that this smaller workforce is, after BMW's massive investment in a modernised plant on the former Pressed Steel site, producing almost as many cars as Cowley did in its heyday. Dr Sharp had predicted that if the motor industry failed, Oxford could become "a second Jarrow". In fact, although there was alarm at the time about the loss of jobs, the growth as a result of national policy of Oxford's traditional industry of higher education and research, and of businesses associated with this, came to the rescue to maintain local prosperity.

Faced with the decline of the motor industry, the council decided to protect the Morris Motors site for employment-generating uses and slightly modified the policy of restraining employment growth by adding a new exception for science-based industry. This was to encourage new enterprises being spun-off as a result of university scientific research. A science park for such businesses was established at Littlemore. The council also placed increased emphasis on developing tourism, including the university's conference trade.

The pressures for growth, which the planners must still meet, now come mainly from government-backed expansion of university education and research and of the hospitals, especially as the city absent-mindedly acquired a second university in a town that was previously thought to have scarcely room for the expansion of one.

The colleges of Oxford University have had a good record of adding, with a few unfortunate exceptions, distinguished new buildings to the city to house a greater proportion of their growing number of students, including some ingenious infill. But the university authorities have done less well. They have twice since the war faced crises over land use planning - in 1962 with the abortive proposal for a zoology tower in the Parks, and in 1996 with the initial plan, later dropped, to put the Said Business School on a site in Mansfield Road which the university had pledged to keep green in perpetuity. The university's new buildings are of mixed quality; the recent one for chemistry is overpoweringly bulky and damages the setting of Mansfield College, a major listed building.

The local development plan recognises that the best answer to the university's need for more space, particularly for research, is for it to acquire, as it recently has done, the land to be released by the move of the Radcliffe Infirmary to Headington, although a third of the site is still being retained for medical use as a local health centre. Any land released by the similar move of the Acland Hospital to Headington has also been earmarked for use by the colleges or the university. The city plan as well deliberately permits commercial offices to be acquired for university research and administration.

But if the growth said to be necessary to sustain Oxford's position as a world-class university is to continue, the university will have to decentralise any activities it possibly can. It has already begun to do this with the storage of Bodleian books at Nuneham Courtenay, the development of links with Harwell and Culham, and the creation of a science park at the former weed research station at Begbroke.

The removal of the Infirmary from the Woodstock Road will complete the post-war policy of concentrating Oxford's hospitals, and the research and training of doctors and other medical staff associated with them, in buildings, mostly new, in the Headington area. The latest development is the proposal to create a children's hospital on the John Radcliffe site. All this, however, in its turn threatens to create fresh traffic problems in Headington which are not yet fully resolved.

If the conversion of Oxford's College of Technology into a polytechnic in 1970 had ever been considered as a planning issue, the new institution, now Oxford Brookes, might well have been urged to go to Swindon which was earmarked for growth. Instead it stayed, helped by its location and its innovative modular courses to become the most successful of the new polytechnic-based universities and to contribute to employment. But it has added to the growth pressures in the city, particularly in the housing market, as it has so far been able to do much less than the older university to house its own students.

Fortunately it was able to acquire Headington Hill Hall, next to its main campus, from the council after the collapse of the Maxwell publishing empire. It has with council encouragement also acquired the Government Buildings site in the same area, to which it has just added the former Milham Ford school buildings. It has as well two sites outside the city. The city council rightly wants further growth of numbers to be kept in step with the provision of more student housing.

The green belt policy of restraining the physical growth of the city has been criticised for contributing to the high house prices in Oxford, to the shortage of affordable housing, and to an increase in commuting and consequent traffic. But it seems unlikely that house prices would have been appreciably reduced or commuting substantially cut by even much larger expansion of the city than has taken place.

The growth of employment opportunities in Oxford, and the continuing recruitment in the 1960s at Cowley in spite of the limits agreed with the council, was bound to encourage the practice of workers travelling in from a wide area. It is not surprising that the 1991 census shows that half the city's working population lived outside its boundaries, especially as these do not include virtual suburbs like Kidlington, Botley, Kennington, Cumnor Hill and Boars Hill. But the long-established policy of employment restraint has operated to prevent an even greater imbalance between housing and jobs. Fears that this policy would stop the city from surmounting successfully the loss of jobs caused by the rundown at Cowley or destroy prosperity have proved unfounded.

In the last few years housebuilding in the city has in fact gone faster than was predicted or required under Government plans. As well as encouraging large-scale housebuilding at Greater Leys, an expansion of Blackbird Leys, the city has been remarkably successful in reusing brownfield land, as firms have moved out of the city, releasing windfall sites, including land most of the way up the canal in North Oxford. There has also been much adaptation and extension, and some replacement, of existing houses.

The trouble is that, as developers know to their profit, Oxford is a desirable city in which to live where demand for housing will always be strong, even attracting commuters to London. The real problem in Oxford, as in other housing hotspots in the South, is that even if far more new houses were built, the market, left to itself, would not provide the affordable social housing which is so badly needed. The planning authority has to develop policies to ensure this, as the council has recognised with its proposals in the draft development plan, with strong support from the public, for one in two new houses to be affordable ones and for special help also for key workers.

Inevitably the immediate effect of establishing the green belt was to increase pressure from developers for housing land in the villages nearest the city, some of which had been designated for limited expansion. But it soon became clear this piecemeal pockmarking of villages was unsatisfactory. Oxfordshire County Council, which became responsible for countywide planning through the structure plan when Oxford ceased to be a county borough in 1974, then decided to try to concentrate development beyond the green belt in the neighbouring county towns - especially in the Oxford context Witney, Didcot and Bicester.

The argument for this is that it makes it easier to improve and encourage the use of public transport links to Oxford and that these towns are more capable of growing as employment and shopping centres in their own right and not just as dormitories for the city. The reality is that Oxford is at the heart of what must be regarded as, and planned for as, a city region.

The ambition, expressed in the 1953 development plan, to prevent the population of the area for which Oxford is the natural centre from increasing was plainly unrealistic. But the policy of setting physical limits to the city's expansion through the green belt and the supporting one of restraining employment growth, have helped to contain the pressures on the historic city and its setting. Without them Oxford could have been far larger, joining up with more of the neighbouring settlements and undermining both their identity and that of the city. Kidlington may be almost a suburb of Oxford but it is still proud of its claim to be the largest village in England.

So far it has proved possible, helped by large shifts over time in the pattern of land use, to provide land within the city for necessary new requirements, particularly for the universities and hospitals. But there is now a danger, reinforced by the current Government emphasis on reusing brownfield land and building at higher densities, that excessive infilling and replacement will erode the fabric of neighbourhoods and damage the interplay of buildings and green spaces that is so much part of the character of Oxford. Buildings outside conservation areas that may not be worth listing nationally, but are of some local merit, need protection.

With the current revision of the city local plan and the county structure plan, planning policy is again under review. There is also the complication that the county is likely to lose most of its planning powers to a remote South-East authority in Guildford. The pressures on Oxford remain formidable, but at least its problems are those of a vibrant city rather than of one that is in decay.

Part I

•••••

Visions for the City's Life

Cornmarket, looking North.
Photo Edmund Gray

Questioning the Growth Assumption

By Mike Woodin

As Oxford stumbles into another millennium it confronts in microcosm many of the problems that afflict society globally. Like the planet, Oxford is a beautiful but rather constrained place; pockets of extreme affluence exist cheek by jowl with some of the most socially excluded areas of the country; its remaining green areas are under constant threat of development; its roads are clogged; its air is polluted.

Much the same could be said of any city in the world, but the outstanding beauty of Oxford's historic core, its narrow lanes and the tightly drawn boundaries of the encircling floodplain bring the competing pressures into sharper focus than is usually the case.

Previous generations had to wrestle with the same problems and we need only wander around the city as it is today to glimpse some of the futures they had in mind. Compare Oxpens with Christ Church Meadow. One a glorious, unimproved meadow framed by mature woodland, rivers and outstanding buildings, the other, an appalling example of urban non-design, worthy of Swindon perhaps, or even New Jersey. Yet the road that gives Oxpens its character was so nearly extended across the meadow.

Contrast Blackbird Leys and the Westgate Centre with Jericho. Why? Many of the people whose 'slums' were cleared to make way for the Westgate Centre moved to new houses on Blackbird Leys. Jericho was next on the list and the city council had already purchased a third of its 'slums' ready for clearance when the vision changed and a delightful mixed neighbourhood was saved for the future. In Jericho, you can stroll round the corner to shop, eat out or visit the cinema. On Blackbird Leys, you must drive to the nearest out-of-town retail shed, take the bus out of the local community or make do with the small parade of shops that serves a population bigger than that of many small market towns.

Doubtless those who defended Christ Church Meadow or argued that the old St Ebbe's should be improved rather than demolished were accused of standing in the way of 'progress', something, of course, that cannot be done. Yet, despite the benefits that 'progress' sometimes brings (bathrooms and front gardens on Blackbird Leys and ten minutes off the journey time from St Aldate's to the Cowley Road), they realised that all too frequently it can sweep everything before it, disregarding the value and character of what it seeks to replace. When that character is obvious, as it is on Christ Church Meadow, they prevailed; when it is intangible and taken for granted, like the life-enhancing community spirit of the Victorian 'slums' in St Ebbe's they failed.

The challenge those brave souls faced in their time has not gone away in ours; it is to give voice to the intangible and to devise ways of delivering the genuine benefits of progress without yielding to its every demand. Those of us who believe that Oxford should be more than a bog-standard city with a heritage theme park in the middle face this challenge no less than those who, on a wider scale, argue that economic globalisation will not deliver an ideal future for the environment or the world's poor. Whether thinking globally or acting locally, the logic is much the same: more is not always better; quality must count for at least as much as quantity in decision makers' minds.

This slightly subtle argument is surprisingly hard to get across, so engrained is the doctrine of economic growth. Take, for example, one reaction to the news that construction work was starting on a new out-of-town leisure complex next to the Kassam Stadium; it was welcome because it would "stimulate the city's economy". I can think of some reasons to welcome the new development. It will widen the choice of leisure pursuits by bringing ten-pin bowling to Oxford. Occasionally all our cinemas are full and some would argue that a better quality of experience is to be had at a multiplex cinema than at the city centre cinemas we already have. Less plausibly, they might claim that there are always so many good films on release at any one time that Oxford needs nine extra screens just to give filmgoers a chance to see all of them.

In my view, all of these factors are outweighed by the development's location on the city's new outer ring road, its surrounding car parks and soulless shed-style architecture that will echo nothing of its host city. This is a development that aims to serve a far wider catchment area than the neighbouring communities of Littlemore and Blackbird Leys. It will increase car-dependency and traffic-related pollution, undermine the city centre with its myriad bus routes as the prime leisure destination and deny any sense of place. Far better to site new leisure attractions on some of the many vacant sites in the west of the city centre, where the case for designing them to resonate with their surroundings would be so obvious that they might end up resembling a building rather than a tin box.

To return to the leisure complex, the revealing first reaction was not about the range and quality of leisure activities on offer in Oxford and their social and environmental impact, but was about how it would make the city's economy bigger, at a time when Oxford had more than full employment and its economy was so buoyant that recruiting and retaining staff was a major problem for every employer in the city. Was it not obvious that people who earn the sort of wages paid to cinema ushers could not afford to live in the city and that the city's economy was so stimulated that traffic and development pressures were spiralling out of control? In short, the development's further stimulation of Oxford's economy was more of a problem than a solution. Maybe, given time, such heretical thoughts would have surfaced but the 'bigger is better – no questions asked' mentality moulded by the recession of the early 1980s has characterised virtually every local politician who has ruled since that time.

But, hang on a minute, I hear you think, it's not that simple. And indeed it is not. Local government does not exist in a vacuum. Central government has been steadily feeding our local growth junkies' habit for decades by doing nothing to counter the incessant drift of the economy towards London and the South East. By 1999, the last year for which figures are available, the average GDP per head in London and the surrounding ring of counties had grown to the point where it was 39% greater than the average for the rest of the country. This trend heightens the pressures that Oxford faces and calls for ever more creative responses.

But if we remember that more is not always better, that quality is at least as important as quantity, what at first appears to be a threat can be turned into an opportunity. The first step is for the local body politic to conjure up the political will and imagination to break from its dependency culture and realise that the city is not hanging on the slender lifeline of the next government handout or the next decision by some remote multinational company to deign to set up shop in our backyard. In a situation where everything and everybody wants to expand in Oxford we are in a position of strength to dictate terms and set the agenda – if only we have enough confidence in the qualities of the city we inhabit. If we want Oxford to survive as a vibrant and inclusive city with its character intact, we must stop trying to do everything and play to its strengths.

So, what does this mean for Oxford's future?

Housing or employment?

Oxford has a chronic housing crisis. It extends far beyond the very visible population of rough sleepers in the city centre. It includes the many families and individuals in temporary accommodation as well as the tens of thousands of securely housed people who cannot afford to buy in Oxford but work here and are forced to commute, put up with dodgy bedsits or pay extortionate rents. The problem is that there are far more jobs in Oxford than there are homes to house the people who work here. Why then does the first key strategic aim of the draft Strategic Vision, which the city council has just released for consultation at the time of writing, pledge to "Create local prosperity and sustain full employment by attracting new companies to Oxford"? Instead, the council, together with other local authorities in the region, should be lobbying the government to redirect economic expansion to the regions that need it, to the cities where row upon row of houses sit empty.

Contrary to both the existing and the new draft local plan, I believe that large industrial sites that become vacant should be turned over to housing, rather than held empty, ready for more inward investment. The redundant part of the old British Leyland site is a case in point. It has sat largely vacant for nearly a decade, ready for more businesses to relocate there, further inflating house prices and traffic levels. Should BMW ever move out of Oxford or Unipart contract its vast site, new homes should be built for Oxford's existing workers, rather than trying to attract new jobs to the city. Recycling large former industrial sites in the city for housing might just save the green belt and other green spaces in the city, such as the Trap Grounds and Warneford Meadow. It will also curb the rash of car-dependent commuter dormitories that are being attached to the market towns on the outer edge of the green belt.

The shortage of brownfield sites for much needed housing development means that the density of development must be increased, particularly near shopping areas and public transport corridors. This, in turn, demands that very high standards of urban design should routinely be met in all new developments.

Under pressure, the city council recently changed its policy on affordable accommodation. It used to take paltry sums of money from developers to fund social housing elsewhere. Now, having won a landmark case in the High Court, it insists that 30% of the units in each development are built as affordable accommodation. This helps to create mixed communities and avoid ghettos of wealth and poverty. But, the proportion of affordable housing must be further increased. Even if it were 100%, we would not supply the unmet demand for affordable accommodation during the lifetime of the new local plan. Here is an instance where we can turn the acute development pressure in Oxford into an opportunity; though the house builders will protest as we demand more public benefit from them, such are their profit margins in Oxford that they will continue to build.

What should Oxford do?

Oxford's history dictates certain roles. It has been an outstanding centre of higher education for nearly a thousand years and, for considerably longer, the commercial, legal and ecclesiastical heart of the surrounding area. Other roles have been grafted on more recently. John Radcliffe laid the foundations of a regional medical centre. William Morris bequeathed an industrial heritage to Oxford. The old university has ensured the city's status as a centre for tourism, publishing, high-tech innovation and the arts. Yet, Oxford is not a big city that can realistically expect to excel in everything. Too often it has failed to decide what it will concentrate on and has ended up attempting to do too much of everything in a very mediocre fashion. Retail is a good example. Here is what the draft local plan has to say on the subject,

> *"It is essential to maintain and enhance the vitality and viability of the city centre for the economic prosperity of Oxford, and to enable it to maintain its competitive position in the sub-regional shopping hierarchy."*

The phrase "vitality and viability" is borrowed from the bit of government planning advice that says retail and commercial leisure development should be concentrated in town centre locations so that they are as accessible as possible by other means of transport than the car. As for Oxford's "position in the sub-regional shopping hierarchy", it is obvious that Oxford should be the main shopping centre for the surrounding area, particularly because it is so well served by buses.

So far so good, but although it makes sense to protect the city centre's retail function, that function must be balanced against competing interests. Unfortunately, balance is not what the local plan has in mind when it states that the retail function of the city centre is essential for the "economic prosperity of Oxford" as a whole, and that its position in the retail hierarchy is "competitive". This is the thinking behind the proposed monolithic extension of the Westgate Centre. Anything Reading, Swindon and Milton Keynes can do, Oxford must fool itself into thinking it can do better, it would seem. Presumably, it was also the thinking behind the architectural devastation that has been visited on Cornmarket and Queen Street. The intricate floor plans of each century's buildings did not suit the modern retailing methods of the next, until in the current century we are left to rue last century's concrete caverns that line both streets. Still, just think how far behind we would be, and how unprosperous, had Oxford's central shopping streets not been gutted of their character!

Why expand the characterless chain-multiple retail outlets in the city centre if shop workers and shoppers alike have to compete on crowded roads on their way into town from Abingdon, Didcot and Witney? Instead, more emphasis should be placed on the network of smaller market town centres throughout the county and the district centres within the city. That way more people would be able to work and shop closer to home and Oxford could curb the worst architectural excesses of the retail industry and create a healthy vibrancy in the city centre outside shopping hours by developing a wider mix of activities in its commercial areas.

What is true of retail is true also of tourism. Clearly Oxford's many beautiful buildings deserve to be widely enjoyed, but when those buildings are obscured by lines of tourist coaches it is time to challenge the assumption that more tourists are automatically better. The city would gain more and suffer less from tourism if it were visited by fewer tourists who stayed in Oxford for longer than the statutory two hours en route to Stratford-upon-Avon. The tourists themselves would also derive greater benefit. But a tourism strategy based on this sort of thinking would involve resisting some tourist industry demands, such as the disfiguration of St. Giles and the endangering of its cyclists to create a coach park. It would also mean learning to live with the fact that Oxford would lose out to other places as a coach day trip destination. In a world where more of whatever is immediately on offer is automatically better, such a strategy will never see the light of day.

What about the local economy beyond shopping and tourism? The main sectors are strong enough to ensure their own survival. Higher education, the health service and local government all look set to stay in one form or another. Problems are more likely to arise in the private sector and it is here where the habit of thinking big is most likely to lead the city astray. The problem was best illustrated at the time when Rover sold the Cowley car plant to BMW. For a short period it looked as if the factory might be closed down. The city council went into over-drive. Meetings were held, seminars arranged, several tiers of the city's senior management became experts in the economics of the global car manufacturing industry. It was as if they genuinely believed that so much huffing and puffing in the town hall would have a significant impact on the decisions of a multinational company that is based in Germany and operates in an industry with vast over-capacity in Europe.

The fact that the plant was saved was due to the fact that the investment it had received from Rover suited BMW's requirements and not to the amount of pointless effort expended in the Economic Development and Chief Executive's departments of the city council. The city council would be much better off spending its time and energy on the little things where its input can make a critical difference, like encouraging small-scale community-based enterprises to get established in the less favoured areas of the city and in tackling the chronic shortage of small business premises. It will, after all, be the locally rooted, diverse small and medium sized business sector, serving genuine local need not the whims of international capital markets, that provides the best insulation from the global downturn if it ever reaches Oxford.

Nevertheless, BMW's arrival safeguarded some 2000 jobs in Oxford, surely an unquestionably good thing? Well, not necessarily, particularly when you recall the recruitment and retention crisis it created for the bus companies and every other local employer of skilled manual workers nor when you consider the alternative uses to which BMW's extensive site could have been put such as housing, including at least 30% social housing. And those same jobs would have been of greater benefit overall if they had gone to a region that needed them, leaving Oxford with a larger supply of the potential electricians, plumbers and builders that it so urgently requires.

Bigger isn't better

Oxford has so many strengths; it is all too easy to take them for granted. Instead we must play to the city's strengths and cherish them. This will help us to create in Oxford a city with sufficient character and self-confidence to discern between different visions of its future and reject those that pay no regard to its past, even when those visions are big.

The Era of the Oxfordshire High-Tech Economy

By Helen Lawton Smith

'To encourage the development of a high wage, high skill, high value added economy which enhances and protects the quality of life of residents of Oxfordshire and enables them to fulfil their potential'

Oxfordshire Economic Strategy

Introduction

The Oxfordshire economy has undergone a considerable transformation since the 1960s. From being both a rural economy and having a car manufacturing industry it is now one of the UK's and Europe's most important centres of innovation. The visual attractiveness of the historic city and the picturesque landscape of the nearby Cotswolds, the high density of research activity and geographical location have combined to bring this about. In the global economy, it matters that the M40 extension in 1991 has placed the county on major transport routes both north and south with easy access to Heathrow and Gatwick airports and Birmingham.

The perception of the county as part of the vibrant South East economy is recent. It is only since the 1970s that the county became firmly in the South East, particularly when it absorbed parts of Berkshire in 1974. It is the northern-most county of the South East England Development Agency (SEEDA) region, one of the eight regional development agencies formed on April 1 1999. However, the county is still functionally and culturally linked to the West Midlands, a link that is likely to become more important as the economy develops. Moreover, links will extend eastward to Cambridgeshire in the technology arc, the result of a series of initiatives to explore the complementarities of the Oxfordshire and Cambridgeshire regions and the places in between. This essential trend towards a more outward looking approach to policy making is reinforced by the reorganisation of some parts of the business support system from one which is county-based to one which covers broader geographical areas.

Yet how will the county look in the future? How will the county be able to balance the growth of the high-tech economy with its significance for the national economy with the pressures created on land, housing and daily life – congestion and pollution? This chapter looks forward to how the Oxfordshire economy is likely to develop, focussing particularly on the high-tech economy, trying to disentangle the rhetoric from the reality.

The workforce

Employment

The economy is booming. Unemployment is at an all time low, running at about 1% in mid-2001. Growth in employment is mainly in the service sector. Public administration, education and health in Oxford city now accounts for around 30% of all jobs (138,000) in the county and manufacturing for some 15% of employment, behind banking, finance and insurance, distribution, hotels and restaurants. The outlook is for more jobs in the service sector and this is likely to cede to more part-time, female oriented employment.

The high skill economy

Oxfordshire has a particularly high concentration of employment in the highly skilled industries of research and development, motor sports, manufacture of medical and precision equipment and advanced engineering. The distribution is uneven throughout the county, with less activity to the north, but more in the city and to the south. The Vale of White Horse has a concentration of government research laboratories including Rutherford Appleton Laboratory, National Radiological Protection Board and UKAEA Harwell. There is also the Institute of Hydrology in the South Oxfordshire District.

Manufacturing

Manufacturing remains an important element in the Oxfordshire economy, particularly in the car industry, which now directly employs over 4000 people in Oxford and in Bicester and Banbury, where automotive components are made. The retention of the Cowley plant by BMW, following the sale of Rover to the Phoenix Group in 2000 to make the new Mini, is causing disruption in the labour market by attracting temporary staff, causing a recruitment crisis for other firms such as bus and taxi companies. This may continue, depending on decisions BMW make on the future of the plant.

Training

The presence of a small but growing number of training programmes is a direct response to demand created by the expansion of the high-tech sector. However, this is considerably underdeveloped, as there are major skill shortages, particularly in science, engineering and information technology.

Final assembly of Morris cars, Cowley Works, 1920s.
Photo courtesy Oxfordshire Photographic Archive

Modern production line of Minis at BMW Cowley, 2003.
Photo courtesy BMW Oxford

Entrepreneurial activity

From the mid-1980s, there was a very significant growth in the number and size of firms, the majority in manufacturing, and an influx of foreign owned firms, such as Sharp's European R&D laboratory and Genentech. The population of high-tech firms grew to match that of Cambridge, largely by local entrepreneurship. At the end of 2001, research undertaken by the Oxfordshire Economic Observatory (OEO) has shown that there were over 1,400 high-tech firms in Oxfordshire, employing some 37,000 people.

Numbers of companies and employees in the Oxfordshire high-tech economy by sector, 2001

Sector	Companies		Employees	
Manufacturing	No.	%	No.	%
Publishing specialist economic	9	0.6	93	0.3
Biotech, pharmaceuticals & medical diagnostics	73	5.2	3,257	8.9
Computer equipment	23	1.6	1,825	5.0
Electrical equipment	14	1.0	657	1.8
Electronic and telecoms equipment	46	3.2	1,550	4.2
Instruments, medical & optical equipment	112	7.9	5,026	13.7
Automotive engineering design	10	0.7	806	2.2
Motor sport	14	1.0	1,697	4.6
Aerospace & related services	12	0.8	840	2.3
Other manufacturing	70	4.9	1,498	4.1
Services				
Telecoms services	30	2.1	2,335	6.4
Software, web, internet & other computer services	635	44.8	7,899	21.5
Other R&D activities	44	3.1	5,907	16.1
Technical consulting & technical testing	317	22.4	3,257	8.9
Other services & support services	8	0.6	35	0.1
Total	1,417	100.0	36,682	100.0

Source: Lawton Smith, H, Glasson, J, Simmie, J, Chadwick, A and Clark, G (2003) Enterprising Oxford: The Growth of the Oxfordshire High-Tech Economy Oxford: Oxfordshire Economic Observatory

This represents around 12% of all employees in the county. At the start of the new millennium, employment in the county's high-tech economy was 60% larger than at the end of the 1980s. Between 1991 and 2000, Oxfordshire experienced a faster rate of growth in high-tech employment than any of the 45 other English counties (or former counties). This compares to some 1,357 firms employing 40,800 in Cambridgeshire by the end of 1999. However, that figure, unlike the Oxfordshire figure does include some Cambridge university departments.

Oxfordshire specialises particularly in bioscience, motor sport, instrumentation and scientific publishing. More recent OEO data shows that the county is one of the leaders in biotech and other bioscience firms. The research axis combines strengths in Oxford University, in departments and in centres funded by charities including the Wellcome Trust for Human Genetics, Oxford Brookes University, the MRC Unit at Harwell, and in drug companies, genetic engineering companies and other bioscience companies including Oxford Bio-Medica, Oxford Gene Technology, Synaptica, Avidex Pharmaceuticals, Oxxon Pharmaccines and Oxford Biosensors.

A sector performing at least as well is the motor sport industry. Production of high performance cars is booming. Oxfordshire is the epicentre of the UK's motor sport industry with 1300 people employed in famous companies such as Williams Grand Prix, Benetton and Lotus with another 3000 employed indirectly in supplier firms in the county. Moreover, a number of the advanced technology firms such as Arvin Exhausts, Celoxica and Excel Logistics Automotives are engaged in the motor trades. This suggests that the county is developing expertise across the board in the motor industry.

An important feature of the high-tech sector as a whole is that it continues the tradition of manufacturing. Even bioscience companies such as Oxford Glycosciences make instruments. A challenge for organisations promoting the high-tech economy is to explore the potential for overlaps between the high-tech firms and those in more traditional sectors. The skills are to some extent transferable.

The growth of the high-tech sector, however, is not without problems. As in Silicon Valley, there is an increasing divergence in incomes between those who are employed directly and indirectly in the high-tech economy, and those who are not. That in itself is economically inefficient as well as being socially divisive. In a report from the Oxfordshire Economic Partnership (OEP) Competitiveness Working Group (2000), the danger was signalled that Oxfordshire's two-speed economy and labour market will diverge, hindering future economic prosperity. It concluded that the county must find ways of enabling the wider, small business community to derive benefits from the success of its high growth, innovative clusters.

Oxford University

Oxford University's influence on the high-tech economy is as an employer, a source of new firms, training and, to a lesser extent, to technology transfer. It contributes to employment, accounting for more than 8% of the total employment in the Local Market Area.

With regard to entrepreneurship, things have changed since 1959 when Sir Martin Wood founded Oxford Instruments. He asked a senior member of his department whether and how he might give the university an equity stake in the company and was advised not to. The university has been identified as Britain's most innovative in a competition organised by Cross Atlantic Capital Partners, venture capital management firm, and Brainspark, the internet incubator. This is due to the activities of ISIS Innovation, the commercial exploitation company founded in 1988.

However, it was not until 1997, when Dr Tim Cook was appointed, that ISIS really began to have an impact on entrepreneurship. ISIS exploits the intellectual property of the university by setting up individual companies using venture capital or development capital funds and takes appropriate steps to assess, protect and market the inventions. The university's equity in the spin-out companies has, according to ISIS Innovation, reached £2 billion, using quoted market capitalisations and investor calculations for unquoted companies.

Overall, Oxford University has been the source of some 60 companies. These are firms formed by graduates, academics and technicians. Oxford Instruments is the most important Oxford University spin-off. According to its website, the company is

> *'recognised as a world leader in several technologies, among others in the application of superconductivity, the creation of low temperatures, the production and detection of X-rays and in neurological measurements. It provides solutions to the scientific, industrial, chemical and healthcare markets. The company has over 1300 employees world-wide'.*

Its contribution to the local economy has been immense. It has spawned a cluster of cryogenics firms through its own spin-off activities forming Oxford Medical Systems in 1976 and Oxford Magnet Technology in 1984, and as a result of firms such as AS Scientific and Magnex being formed by former employees. Its founders, Sir Martin and Lady Wood, established The Oxford Trust (see below). Moreover, former employees are influential within the local research-to-innovation community.

These people maintain contact with each other and are responsible for some of the most innovative approaches to stimulating and supporting enterprise.

Other examples of Oxford University spin-outs include: Oxford Lasers (1977); PowderJect (1993); Mirada Solutions (2001). In sum, Oxford University is likely to have a greater impact on the Oxfordshire

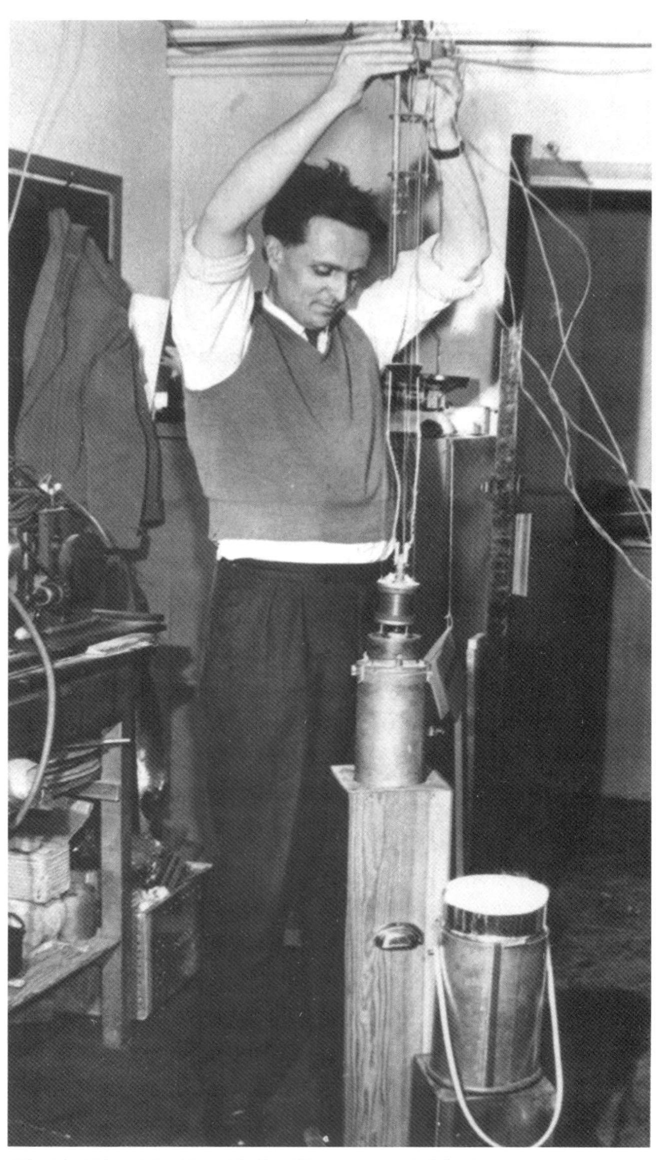

Martin Wood testing Oxford Instruments' first super conducting magnet in 1962. It was the first such magnet to be made outside the USA.
Photo Oxford Mail & Times

economy in the future. The university has been changing both internally and externally. It has become a model of the kind of entrepreneurial universities required by the current Labour government.

Innovation support

Oxfordshire is unique in its networks of supporting high-tech firms and the main reason for this is The Oxford Trust set up in 1985 by Sir Martin and Lady Wood, founders of Oxford Instruments. The mission of this charitable trust is 'the encouragement of the study and application of science and technology enterprise'. Its pioneering activities included managing the STEP Centre (start up/incubator units) and facilitating networking through its Innovation Forum, a series of seminars and workshops bringing together individuals and organisations on topics relating to business skills, developments in technology and future market opportunities, and running a schools programme. Since its formation, the trust has taken responsibility for engaging with the high-tech sector and with research, business and public sector organisations. It has also developed links with Cambridge and European centres of innovation. Its spin-off company, Oxford Innovation, is a consultancy firm, specialising in incubator centre management, and was a wholly owned subsidiary until receiving external investment in 2001. The Trust's and Oxford Innovation's other activities provide help and advice to firms applying for government funded awards for innovation in small firms (SMART awards); interim management, mentoring, advice and consultancy, services and premises; management of the Oxfordshire Investment Opportunity Network (OION) in 1994, and most recently leading the Oxfordshire BiotechNet consortium, a DTI initiative, established in 1997.

An interesting and positive trend is that there is more coherence among local players, which potentially will create a more sustainable system. The most important of the newer organisations are the OEP and SEEDA which have the responsibility for 'enabling technology transfer and innovation', and in principle have the funds to do so. The formation of the OEP in early 1998 by a number of key business support organisations, local authorities, academic institutions and Oxfordshire based businesses is evidence of a significant institutional ensemble which has support for innovation as its central objectives.

The district councils have become more active in engaging with the high-tech economy, although some more so than others. For example, Cherwell District emerged in the late 1990s promoting high-tech industry but the South Oxfordshire District Council has had, in the past, a local reputation for discouraging economic development per se. This leads to the issue of where business development has taken place and what the future might be.

Property – science parks and incubators

The first Structure Plan for Oxfordshire was modified in 1987 to allow for science nursery or 'seed-bed' areas to encourage the development of advanced technology enterprise, in so doing formally recognising the interests of the high-tech sector. This enabled the Oxford Science Park to go ahead, on a site which already had permission for industrial activity. While some of the science parks are associated with Oxford University, others including Milton Park, the leading location for high-tech firms, and most of the incubators have been developed independently.

Magdalen Science Park
Photo Edmund Gray

Innovation Centres

The Oxford Trust has pioneered and Oxford Innovation has carried forward the development and management of innovation centres. As a consequence, Oxfordshire has more incubators than any other county in the UK; it currently has 12.

One of the current and longer-term problems is what happens when firms outgrow incubators. Land for larger developments is less easily available in the county. The problems of land shortages for business are more than matched by the shortage of land for housing and rising house prices. Both of these issues require considerable creative strategic thinking so that quality of life issues for all sections of the population are considered. These together with traffic congestion are some of the most serious problems facing the county as a consequence of the buoyant economy.

Of fundamental importance to the growth of the high-tech economy is adequate finance. One of the UK's problems is the under supply of risk capital. Corporate investing in the UK as a whole is very poor. The banks are notoriously risk averse and although the UK's supply of venture capital is increasing, it tends to go into management buy-outs. In Oxfordshire, The Oxford Trust set up the Oxfordshire Investment Opportunity Network (OION) in 1994 in order to overcome the problems of finance for new and growing high-tech firms. In addition there are numerous friends and family members who act as 'business angels' to entrepreneurs.

Challenges for the future

The Oxfordshire economy looks healthy. It is growing in manufacturing and services. It has made the transition from a mainly rural economy with a car industry to one of the UK's leading innovation hotspots. Trends suggest that the pattern of growth will continue over the next twenty years, with the research capacity supported by an increasing range of experts. The challenge is to develop a strategy that incorporates the best interests of Oxfordshire with that of the UK.

First, this requires co-operation at all levels encompassing central government, SEEDA, local authorities, OEP, The Oxford Trust, the universities, the national laboratories, the Chamber of Commerce and individual firms including BMW. Assimilation by Oxford University of people who have worked in industry to manage the change in culture has made possible greater understanding and co-operation with business and industry. More of this needs to happen.

At the same time, it is vitally important that the universities are properly funded by the government to teach and undertake research and that expectations within the local economy of what the universities can deliver in terms of the local economy are realistic. All the universities could do far more training. This is part of the core task of teaching, one which is complementary to rather than a diversion from its other core function – research.

Second, the promotion of the Oxford/Cambridge technology arc and links to other counties are essential if the UK and Europe are to have the same technological capacity and speed of response of firms and support firms as in Silicon Valley.

Major problems specific to the Oxfordshire growing high-tech economy are related to the shortage of property for firms outgrowing incubators, the lack of an IT infrastructure and a national and local problem of a shortage of risk capital. High-tech firms share problems common to other sections of the high costs of housing and traffic congestion. The growth of the high-tech sector has another downside, a polarised economy. What is needed is an integrated approach to addressing these issues led by local politicians who need to be better informed about the nature and consequences of the growth of the high-tech economy.

A vision for Oxfordshire is therefore one in which partnerships are forged between the major players in order to position the Oxfordshire economy not only at the leading edge of technology but as a social, economic and political innovator.

Acknowledgement

The author would like to thank Paul Bradstock, Martin Stott and Dr Michael Halsey for their contributions to this chapter.

Wider Economic Linkages

Interview with Sir Martin Wood
By Michael Havinden, 28/03/02

When you wanted to expand, was it a problem being in Oxford?

Yes, both the city and the university were generally opposed to industry – not the sort of industry I wanted to create – but at that time, 1959, they had no experience of what I was planning.

The city still had some seriously polluting industry near its centre, like the metal foundry off Walton Street, and the Morris Motors Company was close by in Cowley. The image of smoky chimneys and overcrowded roads and human strife was a common perception of industry. The powers that be in Oxford didn't like it and their policy was to constrain it wherever they could. Even within the Clarendon Laboratory, the physics department of the university, most members of staff thought it odd, to say the least, that a tenured colleague should give up his post and try to earn a living in manufacturing industry; "getting grease under his fingernails" was a common way of describing an unsavoury form of work! A number of pointed comments were made to me giving the feeling that I had let the side down but fortunately my academic mentor, Professor Nicholas Kurti, and the head of department, Professor Brebis Bleaney, were genuinely enthusiastic and gave me very real encouragement and help.

I had argued with the city planners that there was a lot of unexploited science and technology within the university, and that it would be to the advantage of the whole county if a new form of science-based industry was encouraged to grow – this was later to be labelled "high-tech". I said that in due course this activity would inevitably move out of Oxford into the peripheral towns and villages, but in the very early stages it would help if there was space for starting up near the centre of the city. Being a keen bicyclist, "within bicycling distance of the university" was a phrase I often used. In the end I got my way and permission to convert a disused slaughterhouse in Summertown was granted, albeit rather grudgingly, only to me personally and for a limited period. But that was all I wanted at that stage. That base in Summertown became the first official premises for Oxford Instruments and later stimulated the idea of incubation centres which we developed in The Oxford Trust.

Does the environment of Oxford help recruit people?

Yes, strongly – at least until people find out about the high cost of housing and the congestion on the roads. It is a very desirable part of the country to live in, very stimulating in terms of industrial, professional, academic, intellectual and artistic activities. Both the city and the countryside are well known for their beauty, but you have to have a roof over your head and cost is now a serious deterrent. In the long term, a partial solution for the growing high-tech industry may come through a new form of partnering, in which new companies which start up in the innovative, entrepreneurial culture of Oxfordshire, later set up affiliated operations in other parts of the country where there is more space, cheaper housing and less congested roads.

Of course, there would be problems in any particular case, but if such partnerships were to be encouraged, I'm sure there would be successes. I've discussed the concept with a few people who are trying to graft the dynamic of modern industry into the neighbourhoods of new exciting university towns where the old industry has died around them. There are big opportunities here and the need for more cross talk. It takes time.

And what is your vision for the longer-term future?

My vision is of a county where the new sits well with the old. Where the new powerful engines of economic and social progress and environmental monitoring will be integrated constructively with the older traditional institutions and activities, which have made Oxfordshire such a special place down the centuries. Among the new developments, I think of the unique array of modern research laboratories, both within the universities and many others sited about the county. I think of the burgeoning high-tech sector of industry which relates to these laboratories and I think of the modern communication systems and service industries. Among the important traditional institutions and activities, I think of the universities, the colleges, the non-scientific departments, the culture of intellectual curiosity, the old professional institutions, the old systems of land use and the old culture of traditional manufacturing. Usually bringing new activities in alongside traditional ones leads to conflict and takes a long time. My vision requires positive networking and collaboration between the old and the new, so as to maximise the overall gains for the people of the county. I would like to see Oxfordshire become a model in this respect and also for its care for the environment in the widest sense of the word.

You may say that this is asking a lot, but you did ask for my vision.

HRH Queen Elizabeth the Queen Mother feeling the tug of a magnet on an iron chain - at a Royal Society Industrial Soirée with Sir Martin Wood.
Photo courtesy Sir Martin Wood

A Good Shopping City

By Moyra Haynes

There have always been two schools of thought about Oxford as a shopping centre. On the one hand are those who wish to see it as a quiet university town of bookshops and peaceful streets and lanes with old pubs where newspapers are laid out for reading. The other lobby sees it as a thriving regional shopping centre attracting customers from all over the county with a lively nightlife. This group think in terms of footfall and rental levels whereas the other measures success by the number of small specialist shops and room for the natives on the pavements.

There is no doubt that Oxford used to be a much quieter place than it is now, though I suspect never as quiet as older residents like to think. It has always been much closer to the centre of things than Cambridge, with its good communication to London and its place on the tourist main routes, but over the years it has kicked and screamed all the way into making overdue changes and then done them badly. The current railway station and the destruction of St. Ebbe's are just two examples. Decisions which have to be taken now are of the same importance and will influence the whole way the city develops - into a time capsule, a poor relation of Milton Keynes or a major historic centre of learning which is also a magnet for the arts and for shoppers. This last is the vision I should like to see become reality.

There are plans afoot to pedestrianise more of the city centre, to extend and refurbish the Westgate Centre and to move and enlarge the railway station; in conjunction with this there ought to be plans to move the bus station next door to it so that transport can be properly connected. Assuming that most of us would favour keeping as many small shops as possible along with the major stores like Marks and Spencer, the good art galleries, theatres and cinemas which need audiences, then how are we going to do it?

There are some very concrete parameters:

1. Not enough people actually live inside the city boundary to support the arts and specialist shops so county folk must be encouraged to come in on a regular basis.

2. Tourists are going to come anyway so there must be room for them to wander round as well as facilities for eating and sleeping.

3. There is not enough room for unlimited numbers of cars so public transport must be as cheap and convenient as possible.

4. There should be planned provision for tourist coaches with proper facilities and if necessary electric shuttles to bring visitors to the city centre.

5. The town should be as smart as the gown; pavements uncluttered, bus shelters and street furniture elegant, graffiti short-lived, information easy to find and delivery services plentiful to compensate for the pedestrianised streets. More than anything, the place as a whole should be welcoming! The city hosts idea was perhaps too brash but something along those lines is needed; the security guards in the Westgate Centre are already seen as sources of information by the public and perhaps more dual purpose people could be added for the rest of the city centre.

6. There is already a welcome move towards more housing in the city centre as old industrial sites close. These new inhabitants will need food shops, newsagents, facilities such as doctors and dentists. The Covered Market has its great opportunity in the need to cater for the new population of St Ebbe's and St Thomas's. Boots has already revamped its Cornmarket store to include dentistry and chiropody. Delivery services and adjustable shop hours will become increasingly important.

7. Another important strand in any moves to upgrade the city centre is the provision of more protected space. The British climate is not often conducive to sitting outside sipping a coffee or aperitif. For instance, the new American bookstore, Borders, has thought laterally and opened up their cafe where it has access to the outdoors. The major theatre in the town occupies the other side of the same insalubrious alley. There ought to be a glass roof two or three floors above so that the notoriously cramped foyer of the New Theatre is immediately doubled in size even when it is raining. What is now a dirty lane could become a pleasant airy space protected from the weather.

If these pointers were followed up vigorously, then Oxford could become a much more attractive place to shop, to eat, to see a show or a film.

It is difficult, however, to have an optimistic vision of Oxford in 10 years' time because of all the competing claims for space and the different priorities of various groups. It would be good to see the local authorities and the colleges who own the Covered Market and so many of the central shops working imaginatively together to improve the selection of smaller specialist shops. This would be tricky because of the pressure on retail space in the city centre and the heavy purses of some of the big chain stores. In this context perhaps an extension to the Westgate Centre would be a good thing, accommodating the formulaic chain stores and leaving the smaller premises to local entrepreneurs and old family firms. Ideally, of course, there would be a preservation order on Gills, the ironmongers, its shop, its merchandise and its staff.

In twenty years or more who can say? We may all be shopping on the internet but somehow I doubt it. There is nothing like the pleasure of leafing through a real book to decide if you want to read it, finding that you can get into a dress a size down or seeing just the shoes you wanted as you were shopping for something completely different. Buying services such as travel or banking is a different proposition because information and convenience, not physical goods, are what are being sold. Even so, interacting with other people is always going to be a more attractive proposition than pressing knobs on a keyboard.

It would be nice to think that Oxford would be a clean lively city with well-designed shopfronts, safe streets at any time of day and no petrol driven traffic in the city centre.

Oxford University - Looking Ahead

By Sir Colin Lucas

Based on a talk given to Oxford Preservation Trust's Annual General Meeting on 10th July 2003.

In this talk, I want to give the broad context which shapes the developments and relationships between the university and the city: to look at what it means to be an international university in what the French would call a provincial capital and how we can live together.

The present context

The Government has recently published a White Paper on student funding and investment in the university infrastructure of the country. In the public debate one hears more sentiment than rationality about getting students to fund their education. In the past, there were only 35 years when students were fully paid for from public funds. All universities now have to face the issue of the state not paying the full cost of providing undergraduate and postgraduate courses. In our case, the underpayment is £23m per year, so we need to earn this just to maintain our current teaching commitments before we can consider any further development or innovation. The Government is concerned about how the effect of paying fees adds to students' overall bills and their accumulated debt on graduation. A university degree conveys social advantages, and it is felt important that this ladder of opportunity should be available to all. How does one keep universities cheap enough so that the funding gap remains manageable, whilst maintaining the quality of the scientific research which is regarded as a principal driver of the economy? In all fields, the university's role must nevertheless remain to create new knowledge and to transmit this to the next generation.

Oxford is unquestionably a world class university

How do we know? We can listen to those outside this country and look at the quality of those with whom we co-operate. Princeton, for example, welcomes the exchanges we have with them. Analysis of citation indices (which record the origins of other research publications quoted in new work) shows that, apart from six or eight institutions in the USA, no one else comes close to Oxford and Cambridge. We are ranked in the top ten of the world and first class academics and students come here as a result. In the United Kingdom, we earn more in research grants and contracts than any other establishments. We are way ahead of other universities in our numbers of Fellows of the Royal Society and the British Academy, and the quality of our research is most highly rated in all peer group assessments.

It is this quality of research which in the last 30 years has become the defining quality of a university, but of course we have to transmit the knowledge derived from that research, and so must be careful to maintain the balance between our teaching and research activities.

How do we remain in the top league?

We have to continue to attract first rate staff and students in competition with United States' universities, but leading science research is enormously expensive and the major universities in the USA enjoy far greater endowments than ours. There is no point, even if we wished to, in increasing the number of undergraduate students, as each one is already a financial loss to the university. Perhaps we might alter the balance somewhat by adding some more postgraduates - this is a current topic of debate - but all the top ten universities round the world are reasonably small. Princeton, for example, has only some 6,000 students compared to our 17,000, so we are unlikely to grow more than a little. We might also find ourselves taking a slightly higher percentage of overseas students than at present (the London School of Economics, for example, has an overseas student population of 64% of its total numbers), partly because of financial pressures and partly because there is a lower surge of applications from Britain than from some other countries. However, I would not expect the character of the university to change significantly in this respect.

The challenge is rather to maintain the quality of provision for our existing numbers of students, and for this we need to be constantly refurbishing and modernising our existing facilities, particularly the laboratories and libraries. We have recently spent £200m on refurbishment of facilities and another £250m on new buildings, the results of which are very evident in the science area. It is only in this way that we can continue to attract the first rate academics who in their turn will attract the first rate students.

In any event, there is a further limit to the university's growth. There is very little available space remaining within the city for further expansion, the Radcliffe Infirmary being the last remaining site of any size. This will be developed as a low impact site, principally for the Humanities, in a sensitive way in keeping with the old buildings, and there will be some mixed use in conjunction with local interests. We are very mindful of the needs and requirements of the city and its traffic problems, so pedestrian and public transport access will be encouraged, aided by the proximity to good bus routes. The high house prices within the city force many university members to live further afield and travel daily.

The continuing demand for new science research facilities will have to be met outside the city centre. There is some scope for further medical related research in Headington, but the majority of new development will have to be outside the ring road - at Begbroke, the Magdalen Science Park and through closer collaboration with the national facilities at the Rutherford Appleton Laboratory. There will also have to be more collaboration with other universities, particularly in the north of England, and in Europe. Only in this way can we limit the impact on the historic city.

A national university

As a national university, we have to follow the impetus of central government. We are expected to be drivers of the local and national economy, and to achieve this by co-operation with regional and national industries. The programme of studies we offer needs to have some regard for the future jobs which our students will be expected to fill. In addition, in promoting the status of the university education Oxford has an iconic role, and this presents us with a number of problems. The image of Sebastian Flyte still casts a long shadow over the university, and can lead to some awkward relations with both government and media, despite being so out of date.

Naturally we worry about how we are perceived, as people deduce that we actually are as we are portrayed. All our decisions, whether on a change of balance in the student body, a shift in focus of teaching methods, on access or on admissions policy seem subject to limitless outside scrutiny and attention.

A regional university

We have a significant relationship to the activities of the city and the region as a whole. There is an increasing emphasis on the impact of university research and technology transfer to the local economy. Oxford University creates employment for 8% of the county's total workforce, and with the colleges injects almost £500m per year into it. We are a major attraction for inward investment: the university's heritage and cultural resources are very attractive to tourists and visitors, and university research acts as a magnet for high-tech businesses and other enterprises, of which there are now over 2,000 in the county, employing 45,000 people. The two science parks, Begbroke and Magdalen, are leading the way. In the south-east of the county, there is now some feeling of saturation, but there is still space to the north. It is only some 20 minutes' journey to Banbury, we have airports to the north as well as the south-east and a good network of rail links, which admittedly could be further improved. Our business education programmes, aimed partly at a regional and local student base continue to flourish, both at the Said Business School and at Templeton College.

Cultural contribution

The city attracts 7 million tourists each year, spending £350m locally. I like to think they come principally to see us. For local residents too we have much to offer. The Department of Continuing Education offers part-time courses to over 17,000 students, most of whom live within the region, and more highly educated residents tend to insist on higher standards in, for example, local schools. Though Oxford was not chosen as the European Capital of Culture, that does not diminish the university's museums, galleries and libraries. Over one third of the 45,000 registered readers at the Bodleian live within Oxfordshire, as do a third of the 250,000 annual visitors to the Ashmolean and half of the 250,000 visitors, many of them schoolchildren, to the Museum of Natural History. The Botanic Garden is another fine local resource with a significant programme focussing on schools and school children. Although the Sheldonian is probably the most uncomfortable concert hall in Europe, it and the Holywell Music Rooms provide venues for the very wide range of university orchestras and choirs, which play such an important role in the musical life of the city. We are also very pleased to support the Playhouse and all its activities, both financially and through membership of its Board.

The architecture of the university and college buildings is one of the chief features of Oxford and one of the great attractions for visitors and tourists. We are very conscious of our patrimony, and spend over £6m a year on the conservation of buildings within our care. We are very conscious of the need to keep in step with the city in terms of the architectural heritage and future designs. Some of our recent buildings have been controversial, but others, such as the Said Business School and the Rothermere American Institute have won design awards. There are of course tensions for a leading modern university in ancient historic buildings, and there are high transaction costs living in such an environment. The balance between built and unbuilt space has also to be maintained. The Parks, playing fields and Christ Church meadows are vital, not only to the university, but to the city as a whole. In this, as in all other aspects of the university's future, we aim to collaborate with the city and the region, and to maintain as healthy as possible a relationship with them.

A Future for Oxford Brookes University

By Graham Upton

Introduction

In the last ten years, Oxford Brookes has evolved from leading polytechnic into leading new university as confirmed by *The Times*' league tables since 1995. As we move into our second decade, we are poised to become one of the leading universities in the country.

What is distinctive about Oxford Brookes - the quality of teaching, our student-centred flexible approach and our wide and innovative range of degree courses - will remain with us, as we continue to grow and develop in the future. We will offer an expanding portfolio of postgraduate and professional courses, many being developed to meet the needs of local employers and the regional economy. Several of our degree courses are already ranked in the national top ten by subject area and more will certainly be added. We are known for pioneering new degree courses, such as Biotechnology, Motorsport Engineering and Sports and Coaching, and in the future we will add others where necessary to meet the changing needs of the economy.

There will be a gradual steady growth in student numbers in years to come, as we play our part in meeting the Government's national target of providing a university education for 50% of young people. The School of Health Care and Westminster Institute will train more nurses and teachers, helping to meet national shortages in these professions. This growth will not necessarily lead to increased numbers of students on campus, as many more students will join us as distance learners or will sign up for study using e-learning methods.

Further consolidation of our role as a leading university will include forging more partnerships with other education providers in the region, developing closer ties with business and providing more opportunities for study to local people.

We will seek to build on our success and strengthen our position as a modern, student-centred, enterprising institution. We will enhance our contribution to the economic, social and intellectual life of Oxford and the surrounding region. Our vision is that by establishing strong partnerships regionally, nationally and internationally we will bring what is distinctively 'Oxford Brookes' to a wider community.

Rooted in the city

Brookes can trace its origins to the foundation of the Oxford School of Art in 1865, in one room on the ground floor of the Taylor Institution in St Giles. By 1928 it had grown and John Henry Brookes was appointed Vice-Principal of the Oxford City Technical School and Head of the School of Art. He was an outstanding educationalist with a vision of creating an institution to provide opportunities for learning for everyone in the community and was effectively the founder of what is now Oxford Brookes University.

Oxford Polytechnic was created in 1970. It was the first to pioneer the development of the modular course system, since adopted by many other universities across the country. This remains a distinctive aspect of our undergraduate programme and all our undergraduate degree courses are divided into equal-sized units, called modules, with students allowed to choose which topics to study on a term-by-term basis. We offer hundreds of different joint honours combinations, allowing students the flexibility to design a course to meet their needs.

Students can opt for unusual subject combinations, such as History and Electronics or Biology and French, for example. We continue to teach practical and vocational subjects such as computing, engineering, accounting, hotel management, business and building. Our School of Health and Social Care trains nurses, physiotherapists, occupational therapists, social workers and midwives. We have expertise in such fields as ageing and dementia. Brookes now has one of the top-rated fine art departments in the country and we have an equally outstanding reputation in the fields of planning and architecture.

All these developments can be traced back to John Brookes, who set in motion the pioneering transformations that gave rise to the forward-looking institution of today.

I believe that over the next 30 years, Brookes will remain true to this spirit of innovation, offering students a contemporary mix of vocational and academic courses. The emphasis will continue to be on the acquisition of skills rather than on an old-style requirement to absorb large volumes of information. Our courses will equip students with the skills they need to progress their own learning. In fields such as computing and the biosciences, we already find that some year one course content may be rendered obsolete by new developments and research by the time a student reaches year three. We need to be ready to meet the challenge of rapid technological change. We also need to be ready to respond to political change.

Future governments may well instigate major changes in the A-level and degree systems. The nature of the undergraduate degree may change significantly. We already offer a wide range of levels of study, including foundation degrees, conversion courses, postgraduate diplomas and higher degrees by research. In the future, we will certainly offer even more pathways into higher education. Brookes will remain flexible and responsive to change, while maintaining an academic portfolio that is focused towards the professions, employment and continuous professional development, and the promotion of human understanding and creativity.

More than just a university

Brookes aims to be ranked among the top 30 Universities in the country within the next 30 years. Currently we are placed just within the top 50 and we are now starting to outperform some older institutions. However, we consider ourselves more than just an academic institution. We already play a leading role in the socio-economic and cultural development of the communities we serve, and this role will increase in years to come. In 2002, 50% of all students came from within a 50 mile radius of Oxford, 30% from Oxfordshire itself. By the year 2030, these figures are likely to rise to 80 and 50% respectively.

Brookes has always attracted a substantial number of mature students, the majority from the region. Currently, nearly a third of undergraduates are over 30 when they enrol and more than 60% are over 21. The number of applications from mature candidates has been steadily increasing, especially from those living within the region, and I expect this trend to continue.

Brookes will continue to offer the chance of a university education to those who did not go to university straight from school or college. We will always be prepared to consider applications from students without the normal entry requirements if they can demonstrate academic potential. We already work closely with local Access course providers such as Abingdon, Witney and Aylesbury Colleges, offering places on our degree courses to mature students who do not have A-level or GCSE qualifications.

In years to came, as our society grapples with the challenges posed by early retirement, greater leisure time and growing life expectancy, we will be able to offer new opportunities for lifelong study. Through interchange between teachers, students, businesses, public agencies, professional bodies, voluntary organisations and community representatives, Oxford Brookes will be recognised increasingly as more than a university in the traditional sense. I believe we will succeed in breaking down the barriers between education and work by providing flexible and convenient learning opportunities that enhance work and personal prospects, particularly for people in our local region.

The Government wants more students to have what it terms "an experience of higher education". I predict that this will not necessarily be through the continuous expansion of traditional on-campus education. We may offer new forms of fast-track learning programmes or tailor-made degrees designed to meet the needs of different groups of learners. A growing number of Brookes' programmes will be delivered in the community and at work, either through colleges of further education and work-based learning or via the Internet. We will also create new pathways of progression from school through to college and university, allowing young people to build their own portfolio of skills to meet the changing needs of the workplace. We may expand the dedicated part-time routes into higher education as another way of increasing participation among people who might not otherwise consider studying within higher education. In the future, we will be working on a growing range of collaborations with partners in the region and further afield, using our staff and expertise to build new joint courses.

Sports and arts are already highly valued by students and staff. I hope we will see more joint ventures with other local sporting bodies, such as already exists between Brookes and the University of Oxford in the field of cricket. We have recently appointed a full-time arts and culture worker with the aim of encouraging more partnership working between ourselves and other groups in the city. We are likely to see members of Brookes taking a greater lead in the local art and music communities and hosting performances at our venues at Headington Hill and Harcourt Hill. We were one of the four core partners behind Oxford's European Capital of Culture bid for 2008, highlighting how we can play a lead in formulating arts initiatives for the future. There is also a tradition of community volunteering at Brookes. A new project, called STAX, has just been set up, with the aim of helping students and staff to develop their skills and work experience by getting involved in community projects. In 30 years' time, I foresee a very large and dynamic volunteering programme, perhaps linked to other voluntary sector bodies in the region, such as Earthwatch, Sobell House and Oxfam.

Keeping Brookes in business

Looking ahead, I can imagine a time when all young people and adults in our region have knowledge and skills to match the best in the world. That means each person having equal access to education, training and opportunities for lifelong learning both at home and in the community. The Government is expecting universities such as Brookes to play a major part in developing a regional knowledge economy and learning society. The wheels are already in motion and we are working closely with bodies such as the Learning and Skills Council and South East England Development Agency (SEEDA). We will work increasingly with other education providers and organisations to ensure we are meeting the needs of local employers. We will also provide a growing range of research and consultancy services to business, industry and the public sector to stimulate innovation and increase regional competitiveness.

The Oxfordshire region, in common with the South East as a whole, is a service-based economy, with banking, finance, insurance and the public sector accounting for more than half of local jobs. It is forecast that in the near future employment will continue to grow at ten times the national average, with especially strong growth in areas such as construction and health care. Recent studies also identify a critical local skills shortage in management, with many small businesses failing as a result. Developing the skills of managers has been identified as a key economic need for the region. These are all areas where Oxford Brookes can help meet demand, by offering a range of vocationally-focussed undergraduate and postgraduate courses, as well as expertise at research level. The Business School at Wheatley is developing a wide range of management, business and accounting courses, including full-time and part-time MBA programmes for aspiring managers from the UK and overseas. Its Business and Management and Economics departments were top-rated in the 2002 quality assessments and we are among an elite group of universities approved by the Association of MBAs.

Wheatley Campus is rapidly becoming the focus of new business-related ventures. Brookes' departments of Computing and Mathematical Sciences have recently moved into new buildings and will be joined in the near future by Engineering. My vision for Wheatley is that it will become a science and business park, founded on a growing base of research. It has the potential to be developed on fully sustainable lines. There are exciting possibilities for joint projects and new collaborations. We already host many major events for local companies and regional business organisations there. The Enterprise Centre at the Business School, set up in 1999, brings scientists and researchers together with business experts and financiers to give advice to potential new companies starting up at Brookes. Its Developing Management Excellence programme, which offers a web-based management training course, is an example of the shape of things to come. By 2030 we could have an international conference centre to rival London and Birmingham, offering the region a much-needed showcase for its business and research community.

It is estimated that Brookes currently brings £100 million into the local economy every year, and this figure will continue to grow steadily. Already, we have seen the emergence of what some have termed "the knowledge economy" in the region, in which new high-tech businesses are being spun off from research at Oxford University. This process is now gathering momentum at Brookes and we have already seen several spin-off companies launched out of current research, with more to come. I foresee great potential for local industry in areas where Brookes leads the field, such as biosciences, electronics, motorsport engineering and food sciences. The importance of the development of the biotechnology cluster to the regional economy of Oxfordshire has already been monitored by the Oxfordshire Bioscience Network, based at Brookes. The work of scientists, such as Professor Chris Hawes, in genetics, and Professor Jeya Henry, in nutrition, is likely to lead to further exciting new developments.

Locally grounded, globally connected

We have all seen the way in which the Internet has become part of our lives. Brookes has been quick to seize the opportunities this technology offers and find new ways of reaching out into our regional community and beyond.

In the Oxford region, we are forming a growing number of partnerships with schools, colleges and other institutions to ensure that we remain responsive to their needs. For example, we already run a Widening Participation programme to encourage more young people from various communities, including ethnic minorities, to go to university. Brookes recruitment staff give talks in schools and run projects such as "Kids on the Web" to encourage children to find out more about the Internet. In 30 years' time we will be running a far wider range of similar schemes and many schools will have access to learning resources provided by their local university, made available via the Internet.

The same technology will also make Oxford Brookes better known among students abroad. Ten years ago, the proportion of international students at Brookes stood at just under 10%. In 2002, the figure was 13% of the total, with students coming from over 100 different countries. Student mobility within the European Community is set to increase and we will continue to recruit increasing numbers of students from overseas, although many may not actually come to Oxford for long periods.

The on-line MBA, recently launched by the Business School in association with the professional body for accounting, ACCA, has the potential to reach thousands of students, all linked to Brookes via the Internet and more such collaborative and distance learning ventures are planned. Locally, we will link increasingly with employers to provide learning packages for in-service training.

True to the pioneering spirit which has enabled Brookes to see beyond the traditional boundaries of higher education, we will continue to develop an internationally focussed curriculum and to find new ways of creating and using knowledge for all those who can benefit.

The Virtual University

One of the greatest changes we will see in education is the development of the Virtual University. Advances throughout the 1990s have already led to an integration of communications and information technology; and now we have the potential to access data, information and teaching resources rapidly from almost anywhere in the world. In addition, multimedia now embraces video, dynamic graphics, simulation and more. These new techniques are being used to create a virtual learning environment which students can access wherever there is a computer connection.

The days when students were spoon-fed with information have long gone at Brookes, where students are encouraged to learn independently. During the 1980s, we developed module handbooks, which contained all the information relating to the module. This was a first and important step in moving away from "chalk and talk" and making the module a unified learning resource, a self-contained product. This now has the potential to become computer-based and extended to include interactive multimedia learning courseware, linked to the Web.

The Media Workshop, set up at Gipsy Lane in 1999, is now enabling academic staff to develop new course materials, including on-line lecture notes, self-testing question-and-answer sessions and interactive graphics. In the future these are likely to be supplemented by computer-mediated conferencing and small on-line discussion groups, where students are linked together even when they live hundreds of miles apart. The Virtual University will complement conventional face-to-face teaching rather than replace it. It will enable more students to learn via distance learning, with students coming together with tutors perhaps once or twice a year. Campus-based learning will be enhanced, with students able to boost their rate of learning dramatically by supplementing a lecture with online study.

As Brookes now offers over 3,000 undergraduate modules as part of over 120 different degree courses, becoming a Virtual University cannot happen overnight. However, I believe it is not at all fanciful to talk of a cyber campus in 30 years' time where students will be able to tap into the Brookes Experience from anywhere in the country, or indeed, the world.

Brookes University Media Centre, Gipsy Lane Campus.
Courtesy Architects Gotch Saunders & Surridge

The shape of things to come

The Oxford Economic Observatory, a think-tank made up of academics from the School of Planning at Brookes and the School of Geography at Oxford University, is currently focussing its attention on the cluster of high-tech firms and research institutions that help make the regional economy so buoyant. Professor James Simmie, Professor of Innovation and Urban Competitiveness at Brookes, is a Director of the Observatory. He and other academics have identified the kind of infrastructure we need in the region to ensure that its "knowledge economy" continues to thrive. Thanks to its two universities, the Oxford region has the knowledge and expertise required to inspire continued research and development.

However, Professor Simmie and his colleagues warn that the regional economy may run out of steam unless more is done to support the knowledge economy. New and existing business ventures and start-ups require better transport links, more affordable housing for employees and new business parks. There is a strong danger, they warn, of doing nothing in the region, leading to stagnation and to high-tech businesses drifting away to other areas. I am currently chairing the Oxford Community Partnership, set up to examine these kinds of issues and come up with new ideas and ways forward. In the future, we at Brookes will continue to

use our skills and knowledge to help plan a better place to live for everyone in the region.
We have the depth of expertise in our research departments to meet many of the most important challenges of the future. By combining our skills in fields such as business, architecture and town and country planning we can find new ways forward. For example, the new spin-off companies emerging from Oxford and Brookes universities may need easily accessible business parks outside the city. Wheatley is conveniently placed for the M40, M4 and A34 high speed road/rail corridors. It may be possible to meet the concerns of conservationists by creating a new kind of high-tech business park, built on sustainable and ecologically sensitive principles. University academics can work with planners to create places where people want to work and live.

Professor Susan Roaf, of the Department of Architecture, built her first solar house in Oxford in the early 1990s. The house uses photo-electric cells coupled to high-tech regulatory and storage systems to harness the energy of the sun. Despite its obvious advantages, change to this kind of sustainable form of building has been slow. However, I trust that in the future builders will incorporate many more sustainability features in new homes and business premises.

Professor Roaf is one of a team of researchers at OCSD, the Oxford Centre for Sustainable Development, set up at Oxford Brookes in 1999. OCSD consists of four teams of researchers focusing on four key areas: the environment, cities, architecture and technology. By sharing expertise and skills across various disciplines I believe they will develop inspirational ways of tackling such issues as global warming and pollution. Following a European Commission funded study, researchers at OCSD were the first to show how energy use could most efficiently be controlled while maintaining comfort levels in office buildings. Developments of this kind will help the UK to meet its targets for reducing emissions that cause global warming, as laid down by the Rio and Johannesburg summits of 1992 and 2002. Another successful project in the Oxfordshire region has come about through the River Thames Strategy, developed by the School of Planning in partnership with a range of local groups. This set a framework for protection of the river corridor, preventing unfavourable development and flooding, while at the same time realising its potential for recreational use. New wildlife habitats will be created, allowing the river ecosystem to thrive, while maximising the potential of the River Thames for all.

I am proud of the fact that here at Brookes we have researchers and educators with the vision, knowledge and skills to help solve some of the global problems we face as we move into the 21st century. Whether it is planning new towns and villages, launching new business ventures, or spearheading research, we will be able to play a part. At a local level, Brookes' three campuses will be further developed for the benefit of all in the region. Harcourt Hill will become firmly established as a major centre for the training of teachers; Headington will remain the hub of the university and become a growing centre for the arts and humanities and Wheatley will increase its standing as a centre for business expertise.

By the year 2033, Oxford Brookes will have moved on again by as much as it has done in the last 30 years. This will bring enormous benefit to the city and its region. Oxford can be proud of its history and centuries of tradition. Now, as the 21st century unfolds, Oxford is becoming a dynamic centre for innovation, in which Brookes is playing a major role. Exciting times lie ahead and I hope that you will share my vision of the future.

Life in 2033

By Lucy Tennyson

A new way of living

Theo, a research scientist and Nesta, an editor, bought their 4-bedroom house for £2.5 million in 2030, well above the asking price, but worth it, they decided, to move to Bittern Leys. They had lived in Jericho for many years and they loved its old-fashioned movie house, one of the few remaining in the country, but finally the temptation of joining Oxford's pioneering green community proved too much. One thing hasn't changed in 30 years - house prices are still going up. But as they both work in one of the most prosperous regions of the country, they are among the elite who can afford to enter the property market. However, half of the houses built at Bittern Leys aren't for sale, but are offered to local people at reasonable rents through housing co-operatives.

Bittern Leys is sandwiched handily between the region's major science and technology business parks that are home to the city's cluster of international companies. It has a stop on the new hyper-rail that runs from Heathrow Airport via the Thames Valley business artery to Oxford and Swindon. It is also close to the new Otmoor and Chiltern National Park, an area famed for its bird life. The estate takes its name from the bittern, a shy and reclusive heron-like bird that returned to breed on Otmoor's RSPB reserve in 2007 after over a century's absence.

The Eco house in Oxford
Photo courtesy Professor Susan Roaf

During the late 2020s, whole areas of late 20th century energy-inefficient housing known as Blackbird and Greater Leys were pulled down. They were replaced by a pioneering new form of housing first developed by the Department of Architecture at Oxford Brookes University and Theo and Nesta's house was built by Solar Oxford, a spin-off company of Brookes, now one of the country's largest housebuilders. These zero energy houses are entirely powered by the sun and constructed largely out of recycled materials (most of the demolished housing estates were simply recycled into the new development). They also incorporate state of the art computing facilities; many have extra features such as indoor swimming pools, rooftop gardens and conservatories, which have made them the first choice of the Oxford region's professional community.

Theo's sister Sophia is 21 and has just enrolled at university, having spent a couple of years travelling after she left school. Theo and Nesta are on part-time courses to develop their careers and Theo and Sophia's father Richard, who last year retired from his research post at the university, has even joined - as a student this time. At 76 he'll be one of the older ones but by no means the oldest. He now lives in Italy, but plans to study the History of Art as a distance learning student.

Sophia has known all about Oxford Brookes since she was 14, as all schools in the region regularly link up for online tutorials as part of the university's school outreach programme. Brookes has been creating online course materials for degree students since the year 2000, and launched its Virtual School programme in 2012. It proved an instant hit and the school modules are now being used by 15 to 17 year olds across the region.

When Sophia left school, she wasn't sure what she wanted to do, so she opted to work and travel for a couple of years. However, she kept in touch with tutors at Brookes who encouraged her to sample introductory modules from different degree courses. This enabled her to think things over, and find out what course she really wanted to follow. Like her father, she's always been interested in computing, but, as she also enjoys languages, she decided to combine Computing with Chinese for Business. She also plans to improve her Japanese, having spent two years working in Tokyo. Many of her friends will join her as they have all been taking courses at their regional university since they started school.

Learning online

Sophia's school Peers, like all others in the region, is linked into Brookes' Regional Learning Centre, which delivers a vast range of different courses and teaching packages directly via its HSN (high speed network). Back in 2003, only some of Peers pupils went on to university. Now in 2033, over 75% do so, the majority to Brookes. The seeds of change were sown around the turn of the century when the Widening Participation programme was set up to encourage more youngsters to go on to higher education. Students come from all walks of life and the university has been particularly successful in widening its appeal to students from low-income families.

Many of the radical changes in education have been facilitated by new technology. All school pupils in the Oxfordshire region now have full access to all the educational materials they could ever need using online resources. Since she began school at the age of three, Sophia, like all youngsters, has had access to all this information via her own hand-held digital eHub. With it, all the work she has done and every mark she has ever gained, stored in the region's central educational bank, are accessible from home, school or anywhere else.

Once at university, she will be able to take advantage of a huge range of Blended Learning Opportunities, selecting her mode of study to meet her needs. She will switch from on-line and one-to-one tutorials, and self-guided quizzes, to on-campus learning events and in-person workshops. Work won't be quite as structured as at school. Everyone at Peers had to log on at 8 am for the morning message from their head teacher. She would usually do this from home, but some days liked to walk down to the Community

Workstation where she could drink coffee and meet up with friends of all ages who lived nearby, as they worked together on coursework.

Her Mum says that in her day everyone had to be physically present in the classroom by 9 am. This used to create huge traffic jams throughout Oxford, as parents drove their offspring in cars around the city. Sophia didn't quite know whether she was having her leg pulled or not, it sounded such a ridiculous idea.

Something else Sophia found hard to believe was that students used to run up huge debts during their courses and sometimes find there were no jobs at the end of it all. Back in 2017, Nesta had gone to university straight from school at 18, leaving her home in London and had run up debts during her full-time three year course. She told Sophia that they even had to choose their degrees before they knew what kind of employment they were going into. By 2025, all first level degrees were funded by the leading employers, charities and companies of the region. School leavers now tend to find the job they want first or the area of voluntary work they wish to follow, and then choose what to study afterwards. They can change job and change course whenever they want to. They can also opt out of employment, or even become a full-time student, although the latter has become less and less common.

Medical Research in Oxford

By Sir David Weatherall

Visitors to Oxford Radcliffe Infirmary will notice that near the entrance there is a plaque on the wall which commemorates the day in 1941 when a patient at the hospital received the first ever dose of penicillin for treatment of a severe infection. This remarkable achievement reflects a distinguished record in medical research in Oxford stretching back over many centuries. Since the Second World War the Medical School at the University of Oxford has been one of the leading centres in the country and internationally for training doctors, patient care and medical research.

Future plans and priorities for the development of medical research in Oxford cover a very broad range of activities, encompassing some of the remarkable developments in human biology which will, in the longer term, have enormous potential for the betterment of human health. Research is carried out in some of the university science departments in the Parks Road area and on the Headington site at the John Radcliffe Hospital, Churchill Hospital and the Nuffield Orthopaedic Centre. In addition to the university clinical departments, the Headington sites also contain two large research institutes, the Weatherall Institute of Molecular Medicine and the Wellcome Trust Centre for Human Genetics.

Proposed Epidemiology Building at the Churchill Hospital site
Courtesy Nicholas Hare Architects, London

Work in the basic clinical sciences uses the tools of molecular and cell biology and genomics to analyse the basis for human disease. Work in this field will be greatly strengthened by close ties with the new synchrotron facility at Harwell. Plans are also well advanced for the establishment of major centres for both research and the better clinical management of cancer and diabetes. Strong programmes in clinical research are already developed for the study of heart disease, bowel disease and infectious disease. The Medical School will also expand its extremely successful epidemiological programmes, which started with the discovery that many important diseases are related to tobacco consumption, and which now have major international collaborations for relating a wide variety of environmental risk factors to disease. The Medical School also has an extremely strong clinical trials programme which both designs and executes large scale patient trials to determine the efficacy of a variety of different forms of treatment. Oxford has also been a major pioneer in evolving close ties with developing countries and has at least three permanent overseas field stations which are carrying out valuable work in improving their health. It plans to expand its international programmes to establish a major centre for international health.

The Oxford Medical School is also very aware of the importance of transmitting knowledge obtained from both basic and clinical research as quickly as possible for the betterment of patient care. It has an active and expanding Department of Primary Care which carries out a wide variety of research relating to the provision of healthcare in the community. Research in the basic science laboratories is being translated for clinical development in a variety of ways. A vaccine centre has been established to carry out preliminary studies of vaccines which are being developed against AIDS, malaria and other common infections. A number of scientists in the School have been involved in start-up companies to develop their discoveries, mainly on the Oxford Science Park. The School also has increasingly close ties with the pharmaceutical industry.

The research, clinical and teaching programmes of the University Medical School, together with those of Oxford Brookes University, combine together to form an extremely strong series of research campuses on the Parks Road and Headington sites in Oxford. They attract more government and charitable funding for research related to health care than any other centre in the United Kingdom. Thus, the provision and research into health care has become a major part of the Oxford scene.

Why is a world class medical research centre of value to the community of Oxford? To succeed it needs to be as proficient at training science or medical students and young doctors, nurses and other health professionals, and in patient care in the hospital and community, as it is in medical research. Young science and medical students provide a stable of researchers for the future, and good clinical and community based research can only be achieved against the background of high standards of patient care. Oxford has attracted an extremely high calibre of medical students and hospital staff and the quality of care in its hospitals is, therefore, equally high. Many of its graduates have stayed on in or near Oxford as general practitioners and, similarly, standards in primary care are also excellent.

Atrium of the proposed Epidemiology Building
Courtesy Nicholas Hare Architects, London

The next century will see major opportunities for the exploitation of discoveries in the laboratory and clinic for patient care and, provided there is sufficient space, increasing opportunities for industrial development based on health-care research. And, of course, as the Medical School increases its international reputation and, in particular, becomes a major centre for world health, it will help to carry the good name of Oxford way beyond the confines of the city, with many potential benefits for its future development.

The Legacy of the Capital of Culture Bid

By Paul Langford

Culture is the creative interaction of human beings to form complex phenomena and forces. Sometimes we use the word primarily to identify the values, customs and manners that define groups of people. Sometimes we use it more narrowly to describe the aesthetic and intellectual achievements that accompany the processes of social formation. Confusion between the two usages is common but understandable. The two processes are, after all, closely associated.

The competition to be European Capital of Culture was mounted by the Department of Culture, Media and Sport (DCMS). It took for granted that culture in the sense of the arts was in itself something that could be analysed both quantitatively and qualitatively. Even then, though, it also assumed that culture so defined was a powerful determinant of social behaviour, economic development and individual improvement. Those of us bidding for the title sometimes felt that Oxford was from the beginning at a disadvantage in this respect. We got the impression that the people of Oxford and Oxfordshire were seen as having too many social and economic advantages already, or alternatively as having social (specifically 'elitist', whatever that means) tendencies of the wrong kind, or lastly as lacking the scale and size to make for a worthy experiment in social development via cultural funding. History will judge, of course.

One thing is clear. Failing to win the title of European Capital of Culture is not going to hold back the processes of change that the years ahead will bring. Oxfordshire is a county of extremely rapid economic growth based to an unusual extent on both technological and cultural innovation. Its demography, settlement patterns and community change will continue to evolve faster than many other counties even in the buoyant south-east of England. Whatever the cultural future holds, it seems reasonable to suppose that change will follow these basic forces.

That is not to say that some things are not long-lasting. The cultural contribution made by the universities is already immense and will certainly not reduce. The performing arts in Oxford are to a considerable extent characterised by the historical pattern developed by a collegiate university at the heart of the city. The range and diversity of musical and dramatic activities would be hard to match anywhere. The ability of a university city to attract performers of national and world class quality ensure that it is not only home-grown and voluntary talent that will be involved. Nor is it only Oxford's academic renown that brings in talents with audiences to match. Communication between Oxford and especially London will remain key to this accessibility. In the visual arts, the creativity that goes with high quality teaching on a large scale at Oxford Brookes and on a smaller scale, but of excellence, in Oxford University will generate continuing work of highly marketable and viewable importance. Both universities play a large part in the culture of letters and publishing that has been one of the formidable strengths of Oxfordshire. This is not just a matter of publishing and presentation, however. Oxford as an engine for the generation of creative literature is exceptionally productive and in some areas, for instance children's literature, without a rival.

Some of the most important changes are those in the city and county as a whole. The reinvention of the ancient centre of Oxford, from the railway station to Carfax, and Folly Bridge to Beaumont Street, is already an alluring prospect. The castle and prison development creates a major tourist attraction and accommodation facility that is paradoxically historic but as yet untapped. Redevelopment of the city's waterways so as to reintroduce a water basin in the heart of the city on the Worcester Street Car Park is a distinct possibility. Redevelopment of the streets within the inner ring road must surely follow the rebuilding of the shopping centre and the increasingly plausible relocation of the railway station. One of the major prospects being worked on is the provision not only of attractive commercial sites for major chains, but of smaller scale workshops, studios and housing for artists. Let us hope that transport development can support this mixed leisure and business area without on the one hand hopelessly constraining and frustrating the consumer, or on the other hand suffocating the life it is meant to support.

The Playhouse is on an upward path of development, combining visits from national companies of the highest quality, with a wide range of indigenous drama. The New Theatre is set to regain its full attraction as a large theatre, with suitably modernised facilities. Whether it will be matched by a modern concert hall to relieve the pressure on Oxford's two ancient music centres, the Sheldonian Theatre and the Holywell Music Room it is hard to say. But the space could be created on the city side of the railway line and it would be sad if the opportunity is missed. At the heart of the city the Town Hall will be refurbished to meet a diversity of needs, exhibiting, performing, entertaining. This underrated and underused Victorian building has the potential to house numerous activities that required a medium-sized auditorium with a number of related activities. Whether the city museum stays where it is can only be guessed at but its potential for illuminating the life of this unique city and building on its underplayed collection strengths is obvious.

The Oxford Playhouse Circle Bar
Photo David Tolley

Oxford is already famous for many of its collections. Modern Art Oxford is one of the most distinguished provincial galleries of its kind. Recent redesign exploits the potential of its present housing to the full. It is hard not to believe that a future stage of development will relocate it in larger and perhaps purpose built surroundings, perhaps also to include a sorely needed exhibition centre for Oxfordshire's own artists. The University's museums, all of national quality, will emerge from the next decade or so with major improvements. The Ashmolean plans extending its usable space by 60% without losing anything of its wonderful façade or moving beyond its current footprint. Pitt Rivers also has plans to provide proper visitor support for this unmatched treasure house of anthropological rarities in an idiosyncratic but endlessly charming galleried hall. In recent years the two remaining museums, the History of Science and Natural History have both hugely improved the quality of their provision. But surely the most significant change of recent years, which lies at the heart of museum and collection strategy in city and universities alike, is the emphasis on accessibility to all. The enormous increase in school usage of these great national centres of exhibiting excellence is a heartening trend that will strengthen.

In Oxford's bid to be European Capital of Culture we were as interested by the city beyond Magdalen Bridge as by the older city and university area. Multicultural development has been a marked feature for some quarter of a century and is unlikely to let up. Two mosques are already under construction. The wealth of cultural traditions on offer not only to those within minority groups but for the public at large in the multiplicity of eating places on the Cowley Road and its tributaries is obvious. A distinctive feature of our bid was our weaving together of social, scientific and cultural creativity in some imaginative festival formats that included major celebrations of Oxfordshire's food, waterways and countryside. East Oxford's numerous projects that mix community improvement with cultural excellence featured much in the bid and will continue to prosper. The Pegasus theatre, a success story waiting for the happy ending of a properly designed and furnished auditorium, is on the way to achieving its desired outcome. Nor should the newness of much that is happening in East Oxford be allowed to obscure the need for innovation beyond its inner districts. In recent years much has been done to improve the large housing estates beyond or only just within the Ring Road that have suffered disproportionately from economic change. Cultural change ought to be able to enhance urban design in terms of the everyday living environment in such places.

As the economic dynamism of the county combines with the preservation of a green belt around Oxford itself, the emphasis on effective county wide transport naturally increases. The new sports and leisure centre at Abingdon is already drawing users from large parts of the city. The market towns or even villages turned modern high-tech industrial centres such as Banbury, Wantage, Henley, Didcot, all boast substantial cultural resources. The full potential of these towns and the surrounding countryside has yet to be fully grasped, especially by tourists, many of whom leave Oxford's dreaming spires without any exposure to the county beyond. Oxfordshire has some of the finest of all English countryside, as yet preciously unspoilt. Three of the country's most impressive scenic assets, the Cotswolds, the Chilterns, the North Wessex Downs meet in this county, unified by the Thames and its valley. Spreading both the burden and the rewards of an internationally renowned tourist attraction to take full advantage of these resources, is in everyone's interest and is already a conscious strategic aim.

Modern Art Oxford, Upper Gallery. 'Male Stripper' by Jim Lambie 2003
Photo David Tolley

Oxford and Oxfordshire have no one festival, like Edinburgh or Bath. What they do have is a great plethora of festivals, which take for granted that this is a remarkable place that can support these celebrations without putting them in what might be the straitjacket of one 'event'. Above all, our central aim in the bid was to have the best of both these worlds, playing to the intrinsic energy and strength of voluntary activity all over the county, but developing the collaborations and marketing potential that might make the whole greater than the combination of its parts. We are still planning on that basis, albeit without the national funding that winning the title might have secured.

In some ways emerging with the title of Centre of Culture (awarded only to the five short-listed cities) frees us from the artificial restrictions of a competition dominated by monolithic Victorian cities. In any event it is the vitality of the communities of Oxfordshire that we seek to support and reinforce. The results will be of very different kinds in all kinds of places. A rural parish fete and the Cowley carnival, or the Oxford Literary Festival and the Cropredy Folk Festival, for instance, rnay seem to have little in common but they are united in a colourful spectrum of cultural pursuits that flourish above all because they spring from inherent enthusiasm and excellence not from externally imposed or forced agendas.

A recent survey showed that Oxford has a higher incidence of cultural activity that any other British city. This is a population of relatively high education and high earning. Yet it must be borne in mind that there are major pockets of social deprivation both in Oxford itself and in other parts of the county. And so we return to the diverse meanings of cultural growth. Social regeneration by cultural means is not as easy as some champions of additional cultural investment wishfully claim. But Oxford has the ideal situation from which to address that challenge. Its peculiar combination of strengths earned high commendation from the DCMS panel: an astonishing heritage site, cultural creativity of great diversity that brought science together with arts, innovation with tradition, city with countryside, and not least international recognition and cosmopolitanism of a kind that no other British city outside London can easily match.

Institutions are not substitutes for people. Oxford Inspires was established to do a job, to bid for the title of European Capital of Culture and to assist with the cultural development of a city region and county that stands as much in need of co-ordinating of ideas and activities as in their generation. It was set up by five bodies, the two universities, the city and county councils and the Arts Council regional authority. The degree of partnership that it represented was strongly commended by the panel of DCMS judges and is rightly seen as something of a historic breakthrough in terms of relationships that have had their problems in the past. Town and gown have not always collaborated closely. One of their most disastrous interactions, nearly eight centuries ago, in 1208, resulted in physical combat and the flight of Oxford scholars to set up the sister University of Cambridge! Local authorities have had their fractious moments too, if not with the same degree of violence, and, in an area that lacks a unitary council, ensuring that they collaborate effectively is vital to us all.

Our stakeholders at present are minded to give Oxford Inspires a continuing role in the festival and cultural development of the city and county. Whatever happens it seems that it will be part of the evolving cultural scene for the foreseeable future.

Front facade of Modern Art Oxford with 'California uber-alles'
by Jake & Dinos Chapman 2003
Photo Steve White Courtesy Modern Art Oxford

Whose Museums are They?

By Keith Thomson

Oxford is blessed with a wider array of museums, and of higher stature, than any city in the land except London. They contain fabulous collections and several are in buildings that are national treasures in themselves. Whose are they? What are they for?

Oxford's museums range from Modern Art Oxford, a private foundation formerly Museum of Modern Art, and the city's own Museum of Oxford to the great museums of the university, (Ashmolean Museum, Oxford University Museum of Natural History, Pitt Rivers Museum and Museum of the History of Science), the Bate Collection of Musical Instruments, the University Botanic Garden and Christ Church Picture Gallery owned by the college. On any given day, a member of the public has the chance to learn about the history of the city or view the greatest works of art from classical to modern times and the finest collections of natural history, anthropology and history of science outside London. And the public do just that; over a million visitors use these institutions every year.

They are all the very best of their kind and, this being Oxford, quite a few of these institutions were the first. The University Botanic Garden is Britain's oldest and the Ashmolean was the world's first university museum to open to the public. The university is very proud of this public access to its collections and buildings but until recently the public might have felt a certain ambiguity - a certain questioning of just how welcome they might be to venture within those slightly forbidding portals. Equally, visitors might have wondered whether there really was a fascinating documentation of the history of the city in the basement of the town hall or whether modern art was really for everyone. All this is changing fast and I am proud to have been part of an opening up, at least of the university's metaphorical doors, and part of a great new accessibility and openness. We know it is working because attendance in the case of the university's institutions has doubled in the last 10 or 12 years.

Museums are not always thought of as witty, but there is a nice line in the Museum of Oxford. As one traces the history of the city from prehistoric times, the thirteenth century and origins of the university are greeted with the banner, "The University - Cuckoo in the Nest". At least I hope it is meant as a witticism. City and university have not always worked happily together but today they do more than ever before. A significant part of the university's commitment to serving the public is centred on opening up its museums and collections in every way possible. They have become a most important window between the university and the community. Of course, the university's museums were founded as, and continue to grow and still flourish as, centres of research and teaching. The trick for the university, then, is to follow a double role - scholarly and public.

But this is a challenge for any museum; on the one hand it must not just promote but actively participate in the development of the artistic or scientific endeavour. The behind-the-scene intellectual work and the front-of-house public work are but two sides of the same coin. When Modern Art Oxford recently reopened its premises on Pembroke Street, it did so with what some might consider a difficult artist, Tracey Emin, who is popular in the sense of always being in the news but not easy to understand. "Is this art?" is the question that hovers over so much of the new British school(s) of art. But we should never fall into the trap of thinking that any kind of serious work in art or science is something for "other people". The Botanic

Garden has many beds laid out in scientific order and not everyone will think it necessary to grow every known species of the family Euphorbiaceae (spurges) but the skilled staff of the garden constantly develop new ways of interpreting plant science to families and children as well as expert botanists. Similarly, the Pitt Rivers is vastly more than the shrunken heads, the University Museum more than dinosaurs, the Ashmolean more than lovely pictures.

One of the most familiar caricatures of museums is that 95% of their collections is not on display, but hidden in inaccessible storerooms, usually it is imagined in a dusty attic or the basement. And this charge usually goes with the nagging feeling that museums are somehow not working for the public good. As usual, this is only partly right. Modern Art Oxford has very limited collections and nearly everything the Museum of Oxford has is on display and a good deal of that is on loan from the university and the colleges. But the main university collections exceed six million objects and obviously they are not all on display. Nor should they be because the vast majority are objects collected for their scholarly value rather than for display.

We can take the example of Palaeolithic hand axes, of which there is an abundance in Oxford collections. One might think that one or two perfect hand-axes would be all that a museum needs. However, if you have lots of hand-axes, especially if some are from the same site and paradoxically even more usefully if they are broken or include the chips left from when they were made, suddenly one can discover how the craftsman worked, how each stroke was shaped and how mistakes were made. One can tell this craftsman's work from another's. And so on. One painting by a particular artist is a delight; several constitute a study. How did he or she change brushwork over time or react to changing fashions, different materials? In this way the apparently static objects become under study a living record. The collections of a big museum therefore represent a vast resource for further study. They cannot all be on view although the displays are created on the basis of the knowledge they represent. And they are all accessible on request.

But then, who is going to dare to make the request? Even a keen amateur student of, say John Ruskin or British fossils, might hesitate before asking to see the reserve collections at the Ashmolean or University Museum. One solution to this is to make these vast collections accessible via the world-wide-web. Anyone who logs on to www.ox.ac.uk will be led as far as they care to go into the inner sanctums of the museums' collections. They will also find a huge array of pages, including games and puzzles, created for schools, families and children. The virtual visitor can search the data-bases for a range of information that far exceeds what is available on any given day in the real museum. But there is a hidden agenda in these on-line experiences. They are not meant as a substitute for a visit to the museum; they are designed in part to make a personal visit even more attractive. Information is one thing, but there is no substitute for the real thing. The real thing is what museums are for, not light shows and endless television screens. There are some exceptions, of course. Casts of unique objects like great sculptures or dinosaurs allow a broad level of access but no-one would go to a museum to see a photograph of the Mona Lisa. Museums basically exist to collect, hold and use the real thing.

Philosophically, many and perhaps even most people would argue that the great works of art and science, our cultural heritage, should be in the public domain. And this brings us back to the initial question, whose museums are they? Whose objects are they? The traditional answer is that museums hold their collections in public trust. They carefully preserve the nation's and the world's cultural heritage and use those objects as carefully and openly as they can for the benefit of the public. In the case of the national museums like the

British Museum, the institution is itself owned by the people, via the government. In the case of private institutions like the University of Oxford, the sense of public ownership is more a moral one. Most museums are supported to a considerable extent by public funds, which clouds the issue, but in any case the moral case is quite clear. All museums hold and use their collections for the public.

The museums in and around Oxford have a special responsibility to serve the residents of the city and region. With a million or so visitors each year, the museums in Oxford would seem to be serving the public well. However, it is not hard to see that the public in this case is not completely representative of the public at large. At a family museum like the University Museum, roughly 15 to 20% of visitors are overseas tourists, 25 % live within the city and another 20% in the county.

Recent addition to Fletcher's House, The Oxfordshire Museum, Woodstock.
Courtesy The Oxfordshire Museum

In the last year, the national museums have largely introduced free admission. As a result admissions have soared but apparently mostly through repeat visitors. The Government's pious hope in mandating free admission was that a broader cross-section of the public would feel able to use our museums. Evidently that has not happened. Oxford's four major museums have always been free and the increase in admissions among local residents has mostly been through repeat visits. That is good, as we have all been pouring a huge effort into improving our displays, extending visiting hours and making our buildings more accessible in every way.

The real challenge is to attract to our museums those visitors who have traditionally felt excluded or uninvited, whether socially, culturally or economically and to welcome the whole city without seeming to patronise. One technique has simply been to issue invitations. The University Museum created special Sunday events and sent out postcard invitations to every household in selected postcodes, areas from which our surveys told us people were typically not visiting. The results were most encouraging. Across the city, programmes are also being directed towards special target audiences such as the disabled, refugees and community groups of all kinds.

The answer to the question, therefore, is that these wonderful museums, no matter who owns them, belong to all of us. Measured per capita of population, Oxford has in its museums a set of cultural resources unmatched anywhere in the world. A great deal has changed from the days 350 years ago when the typical visitor to the Ashmolean was an adult member of the university community. Today our museums are full of adults and families, school groups, tourists - and even academics. And this is only the beginning.

The Future of the Ashmolean Museum

By Christopher Brown

The Ashmolean is the single most important museum of art and archaeology in this country outside London and an enormously rich - but underused - cultural resource for Oxford and Oxfordshire. The range and depth of the collections are truly remarkable. Just a few examples will suffice: the collection of Egyptian faience is finer and more extensive than that of the British Museum; the pre-Dynastic Egyptian collection is the envy not just of the British Museum but of the Cairo Museum; the collections of Chinese bronzes, jade and paintings are superb; Oxford and Heraklion are the only places in which the treasures of the Minoan civilisation can be studied; the group of drawings by Raphael and his school is the largest and most important in the world; and the extensive holdings of the Heberden Coin Room are second only in England to the British Museum. There are also outstanding collections of Renaissance bronzes, English silver, Cycladic figurines - the list is endless. And it is important not to forget the Cast Gallery; the Ashmolean boasts one of the finest of all European cast collections, begun in the 17th century and still being added to today. These remarkable collections are housed in a masterpiece of 19th century architecture, Charles Cockerell's great neo-Greek building with its imposing portico which dominates Beaumont Street.

The University of Oxford came to be the guardian of these treasures principally as the result of a series of gifts by alumni and friends of the university over four centuries. The founding gift was the collection given by Elias Ashmole to the university in 1677 on condition that a building was provided to house it. This building, the Old Ashmolean in Broad Street, was opened to the public in 1683. The Ashmolean is, therefore, the oldest public museum in the United Kingdom and one of the oldest in the world.

A museum which does not acquire is a dead museum and the Ashmolean continues to acquire through gift and purchase; in the last three years we have bought, among many others, a portrait drawing of Charles Cockerell by Ingres, a terracota bust of Edward Salter by Michael Rysbrack, a 12th-century Chinese bodhissatva, a major collection of Indo-Scythian coins, a Japanese Kakiemon jar and, perhaps most remarkable of all, a portrait of Giacomo Doria by Titian, purchased at the Luton Hoo sale in 2000 for £2.8 million.

What is the role of the Ashmolean today, both in the university and in the world at large? The Ashmolean plays a key teaching and research role in the university. Members of the staff of the Ashmolean teach in the faculties of Classics, Modern History, Archaeology and Anthropology and Oriental Studies. The teaching, for example, of European prehistory and Islam numismatics depends on the Ashmolean and the planned expansion of the teaching of art history will involve close collaboration between faculty and museum. Research is at a very high level; recent major publications include the catalogue of 19th century French drawings, the catalogue of the Cycladic collections and the continuing multi-volume catalogues of our extensive holdings of Islamic coins. In short, teaching and research are flourishing within the Ashmolean.

My own primary concern, however, as a Director brought in from a great public museum, the National Gallery, is the role of the Ashmolean in the wider community. I believe the Ashmolean can serve the wider community better than it does at present, and by wider community I mean the people of Oxford and Oxfordshire as well as visitors from elsewhere in this country and from abroad. I have extended opening hours - the museum is now open from 10 until 5 on Tuesday until Friday, from 2 until 5 on Sunday and on Thursday evenings during the summer months - and hope to extend them further. The work of the Education Department has been increased and more concerts, lectures, tours and study days are now available to our visitors. The temporary exhibition programme is being developed and recent successes include the work of the

View from south of proposed additions to the Ashmolean Museum, Oxford
Photo courtesy Rick Mather Architects, London

contemporary sculptor and printmaker Ana Maria Pacheco, exhibitions of Brazilian Baroque sculpture and Brazilian photography, Bolognese drawings from the National museum in Stockholm and British illustrators of the Radio Times. More explanatory material, better labelling, better signage, display and lighting and a more comprehensible layout of the collections - these all follow necessarily from a clear commitment to increasing public access. It is my personal belief that museums play a vital role in public education, in particular in lifelong learning and the Ashmolean must be in the forefront.

The Ashmolean must continue to physically expand in order to fulfil these roles. Two great schemes were undertaken by my predecessor: the Forecourt Development, undertaken by the Headley Trust, which gave the museum vital new space and vital new services including a lecture theatre, new workshops, a restaurant and a shop, and the Sunken Court scheme which provided a new gallery for the secondary display of Greek vases and a marvellous gallery for the Japanese collections. Since my arrival in 1998, we have opened two new galleries. The Khoan and Michael Sullivan Gallery of Chinese Paintings is the first gallery in this country to be devoted to Chinese painting and enables us to show our extensive collection of Chinese paintings from the 17th century to the present day. The Sands Gallery is a new gallery to house our twentieth-century art and in particular the recent gift of paintings and drawings by Walter Sickert and his contemporaries from the Christopher Sands Trust. In the Sands Gallery we are experimenting with a touch-screen information system, which will be installed elsewhere if it is thought to be successful. The Fox-Strangways Gallery devoted to our Renaissance collections has been extensively renovated and redecorated and now provides a suitable beginning to the great sequence of our rooms devoted to Western Art.

There has been a great deal of recent activity but there remains much to be done before the Ashmolean serves its many publics - local, national and international - as well as it can. There are a number of formidable difficulties presented by the building itself. Cockerell's original building has been added to in a series of piecemeal campaigns, notably the building of what are virtually sheds by Sir Arthur Evans (at his own expense) to house the archaeological collections in about 1900. There are five particular problems. In the first place, there is not enough space. Many parts of the collection are not on show to the public: for example, only

10% of the Oriental porcelain collections can be displayed. Secondly, navigation around the building is confusing for many of our visitors. Thirdly, a related problem, the present layout makes it difficult to create a route through the collections which presents an even roughly chronological introduction to them. Fourthly, there are areas of the museum which cannot be reached by wheelchair; this will be a legal requirement by 2004. And, finally, there is very little environmental control within the building.

Three years ago I asked Rick Mather Architects to consider these problems and prepare a masterplan for the museum which would tackle them. I hope that this plan, which has now been received, will be the basis of an extensive redevelopment of the museum during the years ahead. It involves substantial rebuilding at the back of Cockerell's magnificent museum, reinstating his original and providing well-lit, environmentally controlled galleries for the archaeological and Oriental collections. There will be a 60% gain in public space as well as new study rooms, storerooms and offices. All this will be done on the same footprint and beneath the existing skyline by excavating the basement and using the existing space more effectively. This development, which will transform the Ashmolean, is in its very earliest stages: the detailed plans are being developed in consultation with the museum staff and the university while the very substantial costs are being analysed. The implementation of the plan will call for substantial public and private support.

My ambitions for the Ashmolean are not modest, nor should they be, as these world-class collections deserve the very best conservation, interpretation and presentation.

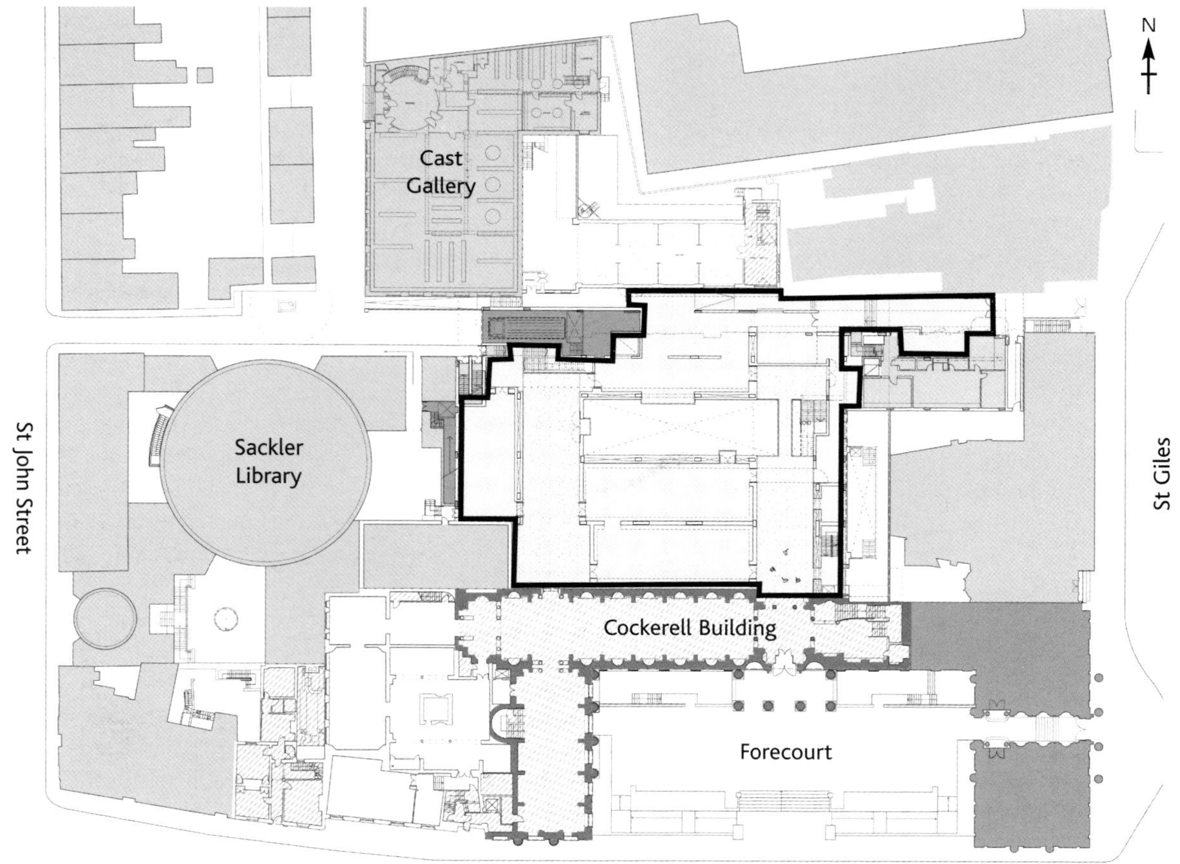

Ground plan for the Ashmolean site, with proposed new buildings shown inside black border
Courtesy Rick Mather Architects, London.

A Regional Centre and the Role of the Public Services

By Martyn Brown

Oxfordshire is, almost by default, a capital of culture; its riches are of international quality and we, the inhabitants of the county, can enjoy them day by day. The task of Oxfordshire's public cultural services must be to work to make these treasures relevant to every individual and every community, to engage and communicate the value of participation and to use our cultural resources collectively for the good of the population. In the affluent society of Oxfordshire today the fears and uncertainties are about loss of identity, loss of community, lack of roots, no sense of place or belonging. Culture and heritage can help to revitalise communities, rural and urban, and bring qualities to people's lives which give them something to enjoy and somewhere to have fun. The value of culture in this sense is immeasurable.

In order to achieve this vision, we must learn from the past, for not all our previous activities have been positive.

An abiding image of the 20th century in Oxford is the final demolition in 1959 of the Cutteslowe Walls, built in 1934 by the Urban Housing Company to divide a relatively prosperous suburb in North Oxford from its less affluent neighbour. Oxford and Oxfordshire have been marked by division. For generations it was the traditional rivalry, occasionally breaking into serious strife, of town versus gown and more recently, city versus county. Today the divisions are much less clear. The old working class suburb of Jericho, built to house the burgeoning staff of the Oxford University Press and the families of college servants, has become a paradise of yuppy bijoux cottages interspersed with upmarket pubs and delicatessen. In the countryside, cottages which Flora Thompson described as miserable hovels fetch prices which exceed proverbial telephone numbers and are now, as often as not, home to commuters who travel to London, Birmingham, Reading or Swindon, as likely as to Oxford or Witney. Young local families are unable to afford to live in their localities and there is a desperate shortage of people willing to work for ordinary wages. Despite the general picture of affluence, pockets of poverty dot the countryside as well as the larger towns; Oxford and Banbury include some seriously deprived wards.

Leisure activities reinforce this picture of division. Oxford provides access to an extraordinarily rich provision of high cultural activity with a vibrant theatre scene, music events to suit every taste, cinemas and more museums of international quality than most capital cities. And London is within easy reach for those willing to jump on a train or coach. However, enjoyment of these facilities requires mobility or cash or both. In towns and villages community arts flourish, but as ever a significant proportion of the population remains untouched. The Millennium OOMF festival was an inspiring example of what can be achieved by a combination of professional direction and community effort; the culminating Morris Minor concert and extraordinary procession of Sellotape lanterns and sculptures was spectacular. Meanwhile, in parts of Oxford disillusioned young people scrawl graffiti or kick the rubbish bins and in the country towns they mooch between pubs and bus stops to pass their evenings.

Too many places lack decent public transport which would allow their populations to enjoy access to the cultural services a few miles down the road. Many public facilities are of poor quality contrasting with the conspicuous prosperity of individual homes and some business premises; private affluence confronts public

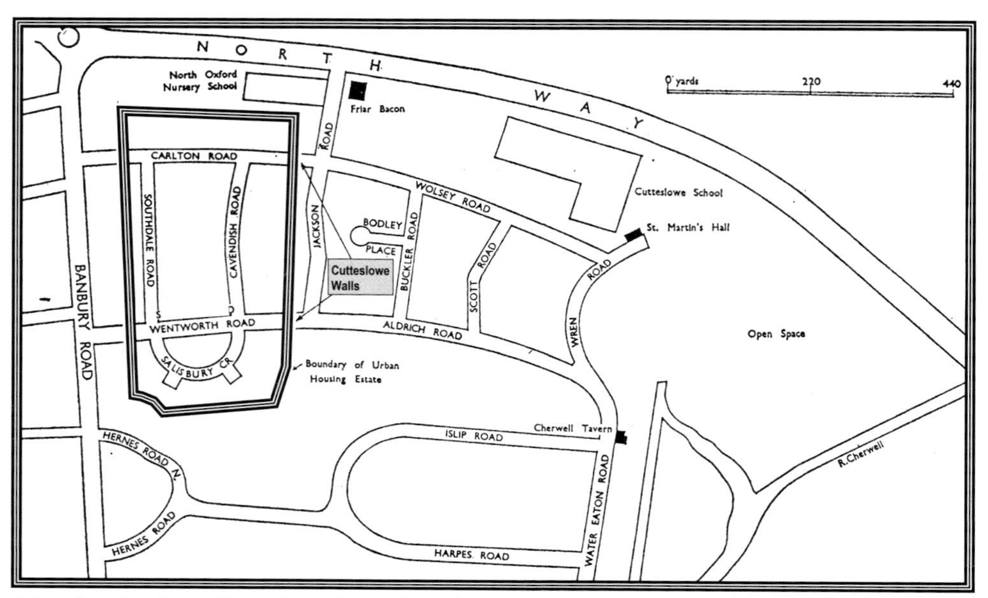

Map showing boundary of the Cutteslowe housing estate.

poverty. For example the public library network lacks premises which meet the national standards for basic floor areas to cater for the needs of local populations and the book stock is woefully unenticing. Meanwhile the new bookshops in Oxford offer late evening opening, coffee shops, comfy chairs, music, poetry readings, lectures and entertainments - and the full stock of current titles.

In such an environment there are clear challenges for leisure and culture. The first point is that quality is paramount; whatever and wherever, second-rate will not do. The second point is that the issue of exclusion must be a high priority, to avoid the increasing danger of a society divided between those who do and those who don't. And the problem is that to some extent these two points are acting against each other. High quality services are generally enabled by charges and income, whilst combating exclusion requires open access for all. Local authorities and public services in particular have to face this dilemma. Their leisure and cultural services are compared alongside the finest of the private facilities and to some extent they are in competition with each other. Somehow these public services must match the quality whilst avoiding exclusivity.

Oxfordshire's public services have exploited new opportunities for external funding to the full. The record of Lottery support in the county is excellent, from the indoor tennis courts and leisure centre in Abingdon to the newly built Banbury Museum, with a host of other projects, small and large in between. At the same time, similar external funding has helped to introduce new initiatives for audience development such as the Access to Oxfordshire project led by the Oxfordshire Museums Council, Parish Packages local history on CD-Rom led by Oxfordshire County Council's Cultural Service and Our Place exhibition led by the Oxfordshire Rural Community Council. Each project and initiative has demonstrated the value of extending and developing services, reaching out to people who may not otherwise know what is available nor how to access whatever 'it' is.

However, the picture is not all rosy. Through the 1990s most of these public services suffered extreme cuts in budgets, typically 30% or 40%. Grants to the arts in general and to community groups were the first to go; then funding to the basic public services - libraries and museums. So the current picture is one of chronic underfunding in these services, temporarily alleviated by capital development grants or short term project funding. This is no way to support services which have the power, to quote the Cultural Strategy for Oxfordshire (Nov 2001), to enrich the lives of everyone living in the county. "Cultural activity affects people's lives individually and collectively in ways which can be far reaching, and the benefits often go beyond the immediate pleasure or satisfaction derived from the activity itself. For example many social, health-related and economic benefits are all outcomes to be legitimately expected from a rich and life-affirming cultural life". Culture, in its broadest sense, is the glue that can mend the rifts in society.

Cultural and leisure opportunities in Oxfordshire's schools have suffered too. Here the Schools Music Service has been under threat and the national curriculum has narrowed choices squeezing out much of the creative and imaginative education that once thrived. The Schools Library Service and Museums Loan Service to schools, both once held in high esteem, ceased to operate due to funding pressures and yet these were the very services that brought an expansion of creativity and imagination to every classroom. In affluent 21st century Oxfordshire every school child must be entitled to a rich and fulfilling cultural experience.

Tourism challenges Oxfordshire. Oxford is a natural honeypot as evidenced by the packed pavements and surfeit of restaurants and yet there seems to be an uncomfortable ambivalence towards these visitors. Rows continue over where and when the coaches should be allowed to park. The lack of modest hotels and tourist facilities results in many visitors spending less than half a day in the city before jumping back aboard their transport and heading off to Stratford or Bath or wherever. The loss of potential income must be colossal. And so much of the heritage of Oxford is hidden; the colleges appear to open their doors reluctantly and the architectural gems and other treasures can easily be missed. Even in the country towns and countryside, the concessions for visitors are few. There is no concerted promotion of the county to visitors, no campaign abroad to shout the delights of Wantage, Witney or Thame. Where is the Betjeman Trail, the Blanket Heritage or John Hampden's helmet?

This is a time of extraordinary opportunities. The differences and ill will of the past must be put behind us; there is a strong vision for moving on. As a Centre of Culture, we have a great opportunity to build on our cultural strengths, to work together, to plan investment and development to harness the energy and creativity of the population, and to move forward to become a vibrant city and region of culture. There is everything to gain and we must make it happen.

Demolition of the Cutteslowe Wall c 1959
Courtesy Oxfordshire Photographic Archive

A Gallery for Local Artists

By Christine Burgess

In 1995, Artweeks, the annual Oxfordshire Visual Arts Festival, was buzzing. At that time, I was chair of Oxford Art Society (OAS), the longest-standing visual arts organisation in Oxford. This society, founded in 1901, regularly holds two exhibitions a year and that year had co-ordinated its members' exhibition with Artweeks in May. Since its inception, OAS had been in the unsettled position of not having a permanent home. However, with the opening of the Central Library at Westgate in 1973, a purpose designed exhibition gallery became available for hire by local artists.

It was there, whilst talking to artists and visitors, that the feeling arose, with the great success of Artweeks, that what Oxford needed was something more than a hire-space. The vision was for a professionally curated public gallery which would be a prestigious amenity for Oxford and a showcase for regional artists and fine craft makers.

Oxford Art Society exhibition.
Photo Christine Burgess

We knew that a number of exhibiting groups, all of a professional standard and showing a wide variety of works, regularly showed at the Central Library. Nine organisations came together and formed Oxford Confederation of Artists and Makers (OXCAM), with the purpose of spearheading a campaign for more spacious facilities in Oxford. These organisations were: Artweeks, Oxford Art Society, Oxford Contemporary Artists, Oxfordshire Craft Guild, Oxford Guild of Weavers, Spinners, Dyers, Oxford Photography, Oxford Printmakers Co-operative, Oxford Scribes and the Embroiderers' Guild (Oxford Branch).

In 1996, two significant events came together. Unexpectedly, the Central Library exhibition gallery was closed down by the county council, because the space was wanted to house computers. This left the local groups with no alternative gallery in Oxford to show their work. Immediately, the artists demonstrated and collected a petition of 3000 signatures which was presented to both the county and city councils requesting permanent exhibition space for the use of local artists. Later in the same year, Oxford Prison closed down and the land was bought back from the Home Office by the county council. As a result of the petition, the need for an exhibition space was recognised and the provision of a gallery was written into the brief for the redevelopment of the castle/prison site.

We are now in 2003 and the position has changed very slowly. OXCAM is grateful to Oxford City Council, which has worked in partnership with the business organisations running the Old Fire Station, to provide the X/Change Gallery, accessed from the bus station, for the use of community artists. This space, opened in 2001, is shared with the OFS Theatre acting groups for rehearsals. However, although light and well refurbished, it is too small for large group exhibitions.

OXCAM believes that in the redevelopment of the castle/prison site, the Heritage Visitors' Centre would still provide the most appropriate opportunity for the sort of gallery we have in mind. However, the developers who plan to convert the bulk of the site into an hotel and the county council's environmental services seem reluctant to promote a dedicated exhibition space at this stage, even though in the Oxford Local Plan Review 2001-2011 the draft development guidelines for the castle/prison site state, "Leisure uses would ... assist in drawing people into the site" and recommends "art galleries and exhibition spaces". The vision - and the need, therefore, - is still there. It is generally agreed that what Oxford requires is something between the Ashmolean Museum which has the university historical collections and Modern Art Oxford which has international modern exhibitions. Part of the problem in Oxford is that it has never had a municipal museum and art gallery. In other cities this usually incorporates a gallery for changing exhibitions so shows can be programmed professionally to promote thematic, educational or local artists' exhibitions. The only purpose designed museum gallery in the county is at the Oxfordshire Museum in Woodstock. Here we have an excellent model, which could be translated to Oxford, either as part of the Heritage Museum at the castle or as part of an expanded Museum of Oxford if it should extend into the Town Hall. However, a much larger gallery than the one at Woodstock would be needed in Oxford.

OXCAM's ideal specification is for a gallery floor area of at least 300 square metres, with top natural light and/or spotlights. It would need auxiliary equipment, such as plinths for sculpture and screens for the supplementary hanging of framed works. To accommodate this equipment, good storage space would be needed. The proximity of toilets would be essential and also a study room to contain slide and video facilities. Ease of access at ground floor level is of prime importance, not only for visitors (including the disabled), but also for artists delivering works.

Oxford Art Society exhibition.
Photo Christine Burgess

An alternative type of venue might be a gallery as part of an arts and/or visitor centre specifically designed to meet the needs of tourists visiting Oxford. This might stand alone or be incorporated into a purpose designed concert hall, for which we know there is also a demand. However, if a gallery were to be included within a concert hall building, it should be a specially designated space, not for instance shared use of a foyer, as this could cause problems of security.

The possibilities are exciting and various. OXCAM and the hundreds of other artists living and working in the Oxford region, look at what other cities have to offer and wonder why Oxford, amazingly, figures so low in public exhibition facilities. Indeed, the gap in provision is officially recognised in the Cultural Strategies of both the county and the city councils, published earlier this year. Further impetus must come from Oxford's Centre of Culture status in 2008. If an imaginative purpose designed gallery, attractive to the people of Oxford and visitors alike, is not a desirable vision for this Centre of Culture, I should be extremely surprised.

Celebration of a Restored Canal Basin

Oxford turns back the clock but not the tide

Mark Davies reports in 2020

History repeated itself in Oxford this week when a flotilla of canal boats entered the newly reopened terminal basin of the Oxford Canal at Hythe Bridge Street. The occasion recaptured the civic pride and excitement witnessed 230 years earlier when completion of the original canal heralded Oxford's first ever reliable supply of coal and manufactured goods. On that day, 1st January 1790, Oxford's weekly newspaper, Jackson's Oxford Journal, observed that when the first coal boat arrived with a band of the Oxfordshire Militia on board, it was greeted by "a vast Concourse of People, with loud Huzzas" and a celebratory ox roast.

Bridge on the Oxford Canal
Photo Edmund Gray

This week pride of place was again given to a coal boat. As many thousands have over time, it was towed under the re-excavated arch beneath Hythe Bridge Street by a single, sturdy horse. In further keeping with precedent, the narrow boat's hold hosted a small military band as well as a dozen or so people descended from traditional boating families who had lived and worked on similar boats in the last century. Another twenty-three boats of vintage manufacture or traditional design followed, each representing a decade of the canal's existence and each with musicians aboard, playing in chronological sequence everything from classical, opera and traditional folk to jazz, rock 'n' roll and 21st century rock. A huge barbecue was provided in place of the ox of 1790 and Oxford's citizens showed their appreciation with "Huzzas" of modern day equivalence.

The Inland Waterways Association and British Waterways (BW) can take joint credit for championing the restored basin. They had promoted the idea for many years before Oxford's shortlisting as a candidate for the 2008 European Capital of Culture provided a new impetus in 2002. Soon after, the site, which had been purchased by Nuffield College in 1937, filled with rubble in the 1950s and filled with cars for much of the intervening period, was made available for the scheme to become a reality. The result is something of which the city can be truly proud, much as when the canal's late 18th century engineers transformed the marshy plot of wasteland called Bossom's Garden into the canal's original terminus.

In keeping with the commercial objectives of the canal's origins, the 21st century basin is ringed not by wharves for coal and other goods, but by attractive, inviting shops and cafes and the stately new hotel and conference centre so much desired in this part of the city. The heritage of the site is aptly commemorated in a second Oxford Museum building, which concentrates on an aspect of Oxford which has all too often been overlooked in the city's enthusiasm for its more famous and glamorous university, the role of the city's early artisans and boatpeople, epitomised by the neighbouring parish of St Thomas. Unlike many waterside developments of the recent past, where harsh lighting has proved unattractive to both humans and wildlife, the night-time illumination is subtle and subdued, while the tasteful use of shrubs, lawns and flowers retains an essence of the ancient Bossom's Garden name. And no canal is complete without its pubs! With their historical names of The Queen's Arms and the Nag's Head reinstated, these two hostelries can no doubt look forward to doing what they were always intended to - catering for a large and lively canal-related clientele.

Of course, Oxford's European Culture bid failed. Oxford had neglected its canal for the best part of 150 years and failed even to show much appreciation of the "liquid 'istory" of its much more famous river Thames. It was therefore always a dubious strategy to make its waterways one of the keystones of the bid and unsurprising that the judges were insufficiently convinced. To be fair, a number of imaginative initiatives were implemented and although BW's Park and Glide commuter service has proved too cumbersome, the co-operatively run boatyard on the canal is a model of its kind. The need for such a facility was obvious - eventually anyway. Smarting from accusations of putting commercial expediency over the very heritage it is supposed to protect, BW finally agreed to retain enough of its historic Jericho boatyard site, which had been sold for housing and a community centre, to enable this constantly busy dry-dock and repair centre to continue and thrive. Its value was not just in catering for local demand but also for the many additional visiting boats the transformed basin is expected to attract. This boatyard, the related Agenda 21 low-impact, affordable, residential moorings, which use wind or solar power for domestic purposes and biodiesel for propulsion, and an ever popular holiday hire fleet all contribute to a canal environment which is as dynamic now as at any time since Oxford's first goods trains heralded the gradual demise of the water transportation trade in the mid-19th century.

The canal is in frequent use as an open air classroom and its ecological value is greater than ever too. This is most notably true in respect of the Trap Grounds nature reserve near Frenchay Road. This rare patch of green amidst the housing which now dominates both banks of the canal was saved from destruction when given common land status in 2005. Already an important wildlife refuge at the time, it is now a sanctuary for many more rare species driven away from our much changed river environment.

Indeed the prospects for the river are considerably less rosy. In 1790 the canal was a catalyst for extensive improvements to the Thames, so giving Oxford an unprecedented, if brief, importance as a trading centre on the shortest navigable route to London. Any hopes the Environment Agency might have had for similar knock-on effects this time round have been scuppered by the seemingly well-established increase in annual rainfall and reckless development on the river's flood plain.

Oxford has a history of flooding and the many braiding streams of the Thames and Cherwell have always been as much a menace to the city as a solace. But serious floods, like those which obliged the inhabitants of St Thomas's regularly to retreat to their upper rooms and move from house to house by boat, occurred only during the winter months. Now flooding is a perpetual fear with the river running so consistently high and fast that there are few opportunities either for navigation on the Thames or to indulge in related pastimes such as fishing or even walking as the towpath has become so damaged. At least, as some former users have observed wryly, this has rid the path of the perpetual hazard of dog fouling. More than one of the Capital of Culture judges, it may be recalled, was less than impressed to find the ample evidence of Oxford's selfish and unthinking dog-emptying fraternity on the soles of their shoes.

Aerial photographic survey of flooded land in Oxford and the Oxford Green Belt on November 10th 2000.
Photos commissioned by Oxford Preservation Trust, with technical assistance supplied by Oxford Scientific Services Ltd.
© Martin Harris for Oxford Preservation Trust

The Culture bid did inspire some worthy initiatives on the river but all were short-lived. Salter Brothers investigated the idea of running commuter boats into the city but the envisaged two new car parks, at Godstow and Redbridge, would by now in any case have been almost perpetually under several feet of water. Indeed the company, which has operated passenger services from Folly Bridge since the 1880s, now finds a season measured in weeks unviable even for their established pleasure trips. Similarly the Glide Friday waterbus tours, covering aspects of Oxford not included in the standard bus and walking tours such as Iffley, Folly Bridge, Osney, Hythe Bridge and Port Meadow, was a scheme which proved to be, as it were, dead in the water. The Alice in Waterland cruises were also innovative and popular, neatly linking the waterways aspect of the Culture bid with the other main theme of children's literature. These guided boat trips to Godstow retraced the route taken by Lewis Carroll on the day when the world famous story was first related to Alice in 1862 and also introduced visitors to some lesser known Oxford lore: St Frideswide's, and indeed Alice's, connection with Binsey; Rosamund the Fair's with Godstow and the more recent plight of the now thrice destroyed Binsey poplars.

But such trips are now impossible for Port Meadow resembles a port rather more than a meadow. The warnings of global warming have not been heeded. The Environment Agency has been half-hearted in its resistance to the planners' incursions into flood-prone land and it is the inhabitants of those historically flood ravaged Oxford suburbs, St Thomas's, Osney, Grandpont, Hinksey and St Ebbe's, who continue to take the brunt of flood waters regularly lapping at their doors.

As ever in this Town and Gown city, the university's lot is a rather different one. The Bodleian body of learning remains on the High and dry while the dreaming spires look down on the streaming mire of the city's "base and brickish skirt" (saturated now to well above the hem!). Some things never change. In the winter of 1767 Jackson's Journal described the fields around Oxford as being "so much overflowed that they resemble final Arms of the Ocean". It is a striking image for a city so far from the nearest coast, and it is apt again today. History has repeated itself to the city's great benefit with the reopening of Bossom's Basin. Other kinds of historical repetition are by no means so welcome.

The Inundation at Oxford - from the Illustrated London News, December 4th 1852.

Sporting Dreams

By John Chipperfield

Oxford United in the Premiership, first-class cricket, a Wimbledon tennis champion, a rugby team in the top flight and an Olympic Gold Medallist. Those are some of my sporting dreams for Oxfordshire, and no doubt, other sporting enthusiasts could add others. But are they likely to happen? Probably not.

The truth is we don't take our sport as seriously as we should. I remember my childhood when you went to school from Monday to Friday to learn and were then expected to turn out for the school rugby or cricket team on Saturday. You felt very uncomfortable if you had to tell the master that you couldn't play. Even a genuine excuse left you embarrassed. You were simply expected to put the school first.

In many schools today, sport appears to be well down the list of priorities. Staff say they are too busy teaching and meeting the demands of the national curriculum and government targets to devote time to sport. Many pupils would prefer to sit in front of a computer than indulge in any strenuous activity. Little wonder that recent surveys have portrayed our youngsters as fat and lazy. They just don't get the exercise that children enjoyed in previous generations.

In some schools, competition is positively discouraged. It is argued that children, labelled as losers in their youth, could be disfigured for the rest of their lives. What claptrap! The effect is that potential sportsmen and women are no longer being produced in many schools. This must have a long-term effect on our sporting performances at local, national and international level.

We are already suffering from lack of training and investment in our future sports stars. Tim Henman, who hails from Weston-on-the-Green, has been our leading tennis star since the mid-1990s, but who is likely to succeed him? Tennis followers will tell you that there is no one of his calibre in the wings. Why is it that impoverished nations like Ecuador, Brazil, the Czech Republic and the Ukraine can produce top tennis

Oxford's Kassam Stadium
Photo Edmund Gray

players and we cannot? The last Briton to win the Wimbledon men's singles championship was Fred Perry in 1936. Our last women's champion was Virginia Wade in 1977. Our prospects of repeating those triumphs seem slim.

Our national cricket team, humiliated in Australia in the 2002-3 winter, is also suffering from a dearth of talent. Although club cricket remains a popular summer pastime, not enough promising young players are coming through the system to play at the top level. Even football is not exempt. Thousands of young people enjoy playing and watching soccer every week, but reaching the professional game is a hit-and-miss affair.

Little has been done to establish a system for finding and developing talented players. Often, it is left to a local club manager to recommend a player or for a scout from a top club to spot him. How many good players slip through the net? The Premiership is arguably the world's most exciting league but much of its success has been due to the foreign stars who have been attracted to it. In some teams there is hardly an English name. That may have made the competition the envy of the globe but it has meant that foreign players have taken places that could have been filled with promising English players. And we wonder why the England football team is not as successful on the world stage as we would like? The country which invented football has been overtaken by other nations.

I hope local sport, reported extensively every week in the *Oxford Mail* and its sister newspapers, will continue to flourish, though, given the lethargy of many young people, there must be doubts about the future. The lesson is that if we wish to compete with the best, parents must do more to encourage their children to take up sport and schools must show a more positive attitude. There must also be more sports centres, both indoor and outdoor, catering for all sporting needs, with proper equipment and staff who can provide top-class training.

What I would like to see by the year 2020 is the setting up of a football academy, a cricket academy, tennis academy and so on in every region of the country. They would employ staff to travel around identifying and recruiting promising young players who would then be encouraged to develop their talents to a professional standard under expert tuition. Training would be free, paid for from taxes or sponsorship and the young participants would be paid, on a sliding scale according to age, to encourage them to work hard, reach peak form and enjoy success locally, nationally and internationally.

Some of our cities, including Oxford, have failed miserably to invest in sport. It is scandalous that one of the world's finest university cities, known throughout the world for its academic brilliance, is doing so little to help our future sporting stars. The British Olympic team gave an outstanding performance in the last Games in Sydney and showed what can be achieved. But much of that came from individual endeavour, rather than any great planning by the powers-that-be.

Oxfordshire, of course, has enjoyed many sporting successes in the past, among them Oxford United's rise from obscurity to the old First Division, their famous Milk Cup triumph over Queen's Park Rangers at Wembley in 1986, Roger Bannister's first sub four-minute mile at the Iffley Road running track in 1954, Tim Henman's tennis successes and the triumphs of Olympic oarsmen Matthew Pinsent and Sir Steve Redgrave.

But to repeat those successes and achieve even more, we need greater efforts from everyone, from the Government through all levels of society to the grassroots. The words encouragement, determination, incentive, support and commitment come to mind.

Creating a Community Vision to bring about Positive Change

By Clare Symonds and Charles Parrack

Change can be a difficult thing. People get very worried when confronted with a new development in their area, especially if it is proposed by a large developer. We at Building Alternatives have been working with various communities in Oxford to try to involve them in a positive approach to change in their area. What we have found is that one of the most effective ways for a community to be involved in the process of change and make it beneficial is to create a community vision.

We will describe two projects where we worked with communities in Oxford. One was reactive, a response to a large housing development, and the other proactive, trying to get people to think about what they value, well in advance of any development. As you will see, each has its benefits and drawbacks, but one thing remains constant, the values behind the process, which we think are essential to get a vision that will work.

North Oxford

In 1999, Building Alternatives was approached by people living in boats on the canal. The boaters were concerned about the developments happening along the North Oxford canal side. Two meetings were held (in the pub) about what could be done and the result was two years of consultation and community involvement in negotiations about the canal and its development.

Already there had been much work done by members of the local community who had for years been involved in the protection of the wildlife and green space around the canal. What we set out to do was to create a community vision for the canal side area and to ask as many people as possible who lived in or used the area what they valued about it and what they wanted it to be like. We used 3D models of the area, maps and pictures to stimulate discussion, to help develop an understanding and overview of the area and its surrounds and to gather comments and ideas.

We were surprised and delighted by how many people turned out to the meetings and with their creative responses to the potential for the sites. There were distinctly different groups represented in the area and we were worried about whether we would be able to reach agreement. The most striking difference was between the group of people living in residential narrow boats along the canal and those living in some of the most expensive houses in Oxford bordering the canal.

As we have mentioned, this was a reactive process, a response to a development proposal from a large developer. The response of many communities is just to dig their heels in and say “no” to everything because as we said, change is genuinely threatening. This generally does not work for it is too easily dismissed by the local authority as NIMBY-ism (not in my back yard). A much better response is to try to agree what positive effects this might have on the community and put together a proposal to show developers and the local authority.

In community planning, one of the most important tasks is to make a proposal which has the support of all the various groups in the community. If this is not achieved it is again easily dismissed by developers or local authorities as they will successfully argue that there is disagreement about any proposals. It becomes very difficult to argue against a scheme which has the support of all sections of the community.

Sites for housing along the canal.
Photo © Martin Harris for Oxford Preservation Trust.

And the community must have a very wide definition here for it needs to include both place communities, the people who live or do business there, and also communities of interest, people who come for recreation, wildlife, fishing, cycling or just because they like the place. Sometimes they are difficult to get hold of. In our case the developer tried to argue against the scheme we proposed by saying that we had not contacted one of the most important communities, the people who were going to live in the new houses! We tried to say this was almost impossible, but they did have a point.

The next thing we tried to do was to stop the process being so oppositional. We are sure many people have been involved in the planning process and have experienced the frustration of the public meeting. The developer and local authority sit generally at a raised level at the front of the hall, present the scheme and answer questions. Not quite what one might call dialogue and reinforces the 'us and them' dynamic. It was important to us to get developers and planners involved in our process, so they could see the community was not just Nimbys and also so the community could understand the very real constraints on local authorities and developers.

That was one of the most gratifying things about the whole process. On the whole the community was inclusive, and wanted development, providing it was the right sort of development, which respected the natural surroundings and provided for a mixed, balanced community.

The first consultation exercise we did resulted in a report which outlined people's preferences for the canal. The second report went into more detail specifically about the Unipart site and detailed the community's ideas for the site. The report was shown to the developers and resulted in discussions between them and the community regarding the site and the planning department at Oxford City Council who subsequently used it to inform the design guidance for the site in the local plan.

The process in North Oxford seemed to be very successful and we evaluated what we had done and what aspects had contributed to its success and what we felt could be done better.

Evaluation

We established that there were five main principles to be followed when working with a community to establish a vision for an area. The first of these was inclusiveness. If we were to develop a real community vision we had to include everyone in the process. This means not just the vocal articulate members of the community, but those with a 'soft' voice who may not come to public meetings or workshops, those who may not speak the language (either English or technical jargon) and those, who for physical reasons find it hard to contribute (for some this may be getting off the sofa!).

The second principle was transparency. This means making sure that what people say is accurately represented. This is possibly the hardest principle to work to as everyone has their own views and they are not necessarily the same as our own. However we realised that in effect our role was acting as community advocates and it was crucial for those getting involved to trust that what they were saying would be reproduced accurately.

The third principle is about establishing a consensus, demonstrating to decision makers and whoever is going to use the vision what everyone agrees on and where there are areas of disagreement. The strength of the vision lies in the fact that there might be whole community agreement on an issue which makes it very hard to ignore. The more revealing parts of the vision are those areas where people disagree and these are often the most important issues that are the hardest to solve.

Sustainability is a jargon word much bandied around nowadays, however the meaning behind it is fundamental to establishing a vision. Creating a vision that benefits everyone and the environment now and in the future is more likely not only to impress decision makers but will be more likely to be implemented and will have a lasting effect.

The last and possibly most crucial part to the process is to make it fun. If people are to get involved in strategic policy making (which is in effect what a community vision is) then it has to be in a way that they enjoy. Why should people have to give up their spare time to take part in something if they don't have a good time?

East Oxford

Armed with this agenda we went to East Oxford. This time we were working with and were funded by government regeneration money that is being invested into the area. The advantage of this project was that there was no immediate threat and so the timescale was not as urgent. This meant that getting people involved was harder than when we worked in North Oxford, as people respond better when they perceive somewhere important to them is in danger. However there was more possibility of the results being incorporated into policies and strategies as we were not against time pressure and could work with other partners to their timetable.

We used similar techniques to those we used in North Oxford, only the focus was on a larger area and related to all issues, not specifically a development site. We asked people what they liked or didn't like about East Oxford and how they would improve it for everyone, now and in the future.

Thinking about how we might include everyone we decided upon a variety of workshops and what we called streetwork to attract as many people as possible. We had themed workshops on issues such as traffic and green spaces, but also held workshops with 'hard to reach' groups such as refugees, children and Asian women. We took the results of the workshops, put them on to boards and took them on to the streets. The boards had all the issues and ideas raised in the workshops for example "protect the oak tree in Bartlemas Close" or "provide more affordable housing in the area". People could write their comments and ideas next to the issue and could vote on whether they thought it was a good idea or not.

Six months, 26 workshops and 800 people later, we had over 280 issues and comments. The challenge was to get the issues into an accessible format and feed it back to the community. We produced maps of the area, focused on the priority issues that had come up in the process and tried in some way to include everything that people had said.

Community consultation in East Oxford.
© Al Cane

The biggest challenge was to make the vision happen. How do we translate ideas into action? The key to this was to keep people involved and give them ownership of the maps and results. Part of the idea behind the workshops was to demonstrate how people can get involved and to begin that process.
By producing the results in a very visual way, on maps that were delivered to all the households in the area, we hoped to show people the results of their input and to act as a catalyst for action. We also ensured that the results would be used by as many decision makers and strategic thinkers as possible and produced a report with the results clearly laid out. We used matrices to show how the various issues were linked, who could help with the action and what the first priority steps should be.

Some action has already begun. As a result of one workshop, a residents' association was formed which led to a new feeling of community in the streets involved. Many people have asked us for the results to help them with bids for grants and regeneration funding; others have incorporated them into their own strategies and policies. The key outcome was that the results were used to form the basis of the regeneration strategy which, with the continued support and involvement of the community, may lead to the results becoming a reality.

But the most rewarding part of community visioning was not the results themselves but what was involved in getting those results. Getting to know a wide range of people, understanding their concerns and needs for an area was fascinating and revealing. Many people who came along to workshops made new friends and formed links with other organisations and groups. We found that people were fascinated by the issues and comments that others had made and would spend sometimes hours reading other people's ideas and responding. What better way to communicate thoughts and ideas about your area! Particularly with the East Oxford project, people new to the locality found it a great way to find out what kind of an area they were moving to, whereas some who had lived there for years were amazed at what was available. Creating a community vision is a rewarding and interesting process and although it can at times be difficult to handle the variety of opinions and concerns it is a powerful catalyst for positive change.

Conclusion: empowering your community

So, two community planning projects, one reactive and one proactive. Each has benefits and drawbacks. The reactive response really galvanises support: something is threatening the community right now! We need to act! Money can be quickly raised, people will come to meetings and organise support. The downside is that some of the key decisions may have already been made by the local authority; for example outline planning may already have been granted or there may be specific guidance in the local plan. These decisions are difficult to change, though not impossible. This can lead to disappointment when these facts become known and disenchantment with community planning.

On the other hand, with proactive community planning there are many opportunities to influence the strategic level such as the local plan, design statement, landscape analysis and protection of sensitive environmental sites. But sometimes the support and (wo)manpower is not there. People seem to find it difficult to think into the future and make a vision for their area. We think this is a process of learning; perhaps people just don't know how to think about what things could be like.

Remember, you are the expert in your area; urban designers, architects, transport planners may be very good at what they do, but if they claim to be the experts, take that with a pinch of salt until they prove themselves by genuinely empowering your community to become a beautiful and sustainable place.

And remember the values. Almost every decision you take needs to be questioned. Is it inclusive? Is it transparent? Is there consensus? Is it sustainable? And, is it fun?!

What is Happening Now?

As we write this for publication you might be interested to know what has happened as a result of these community projects.

The canal housing is about two thirds built and the last phase is going through the planning process. For the two thirds that have been built, the community had some effect: better designed green spaces, more wildlife corridor and a friendlier home zone compatible street layout. The design guidance for the last phase, which was produced in consultation with the community, provided guidelines which the developers had to follow and the developers have asked the community to lead the search to decide what form a proposed community hall or community facility should take.

One of the most important things that happened was the developer became much more willing to consult the community. We think they saw benefits in consulting the community first, before going through the planning system, then they would not have to deal with so many objections through the planning process if they had the goodwill of the community at the start.

But the real benefit was the sustainable groups of people that were formed; linked by a network of residents' groups and e-mail lists, they remain active and these networks recently helped to galvanise support to save a much loved green space nearby. We were very pleased to see people from the newly built houses forming a residents' group to join the campaign.

The East Oxford regeneration is proceeding. Money was found from the regeneration funds to hire an urban designer to draw up specific proposals based on the community vision. These were again shown to the community for comment and discussed with transport planners to ensure they were understood and approved by the local authorities.

Now, a community environmental improvements officer post has been created by the regeneration board with the specific task of making things happen. We look forward to seeing the results.

Again our greatest successes here have been the formation of local, neighbourhood groups who are taking on some of the ideas contained in the vision for East Oxford and making them happen themselves. We are sure that these will be the most successful and the most sustainable projects. We may have helped along the way with creating the vision and the regeneration board by employing some experts, but the community had the vision and helped push it through, and they are the ones who will make it work because it is theirs; their visible expression of the kind of community they believe in.

> *'If you want to know how the shoe fits, ask the person who is wearing it, not the one who made it'.*
> Nick Wates in the Community Planning Handbook.

If you would like to see the results of the community vision in North or East Oxford, please contact Building Alternatives on 01865 483216 or look at the website www.oxford.gov.uk/mappingmatters

Mapping Matters

Mapping Matters was a project funded by East Oxford Action, part of the Government's Single Regeneration Budget. It was run by Building Alternatives, which was a collaboration between Clare Symonds, the Agenda 21 officer of Oxford City Council, and Charles Parrack, of Oxford Brookes University. Between September 2000 and June 2001 Mapping Matters worked with a wide range of people in Oxford, asking them what they valued about East Oxford and what they disliked and would like to change.

The message which came out of the consultations was that people who live in and use East Oxford, enjoy it, love it and take pride in it. People expressed concern for vulnerable people in the community, they valued the open and green spaces and took pride in the mix of cultures that exist. They not only thought about their own immediate problems but more widely and for the long term. They took into account how East Oxford could be changed for the better for everyone and the environment.

A map of East Oxford was made with the aim of representing all the comments and views that arose in the consultation, major and minor, and those where there was disagreement and more discussion was required. It was given to people and institutions who make decisions about East Oxford and will be available to anyone who works in the area, uses the area or is interested in moving to East Oxford as a business, resident or visitor. It will be used to help protect what is important to the community by telling decision makers what people value and what resources East Oxford has. It will help improve neglected areas which people identified and give ideas and suggestions for new things which people would like to have. However, Mapping Matters was not just about consultation. It also raised awareness of environmental and social resources in the area and tried to build on these.

A poster was printed on the reverse of the map, and extracts from this are shown on the following pages.

MAPPING MATTERS

EAST OXFORD

We asked you what you wanted for the future of East Oxford and this is what you said...

Putting what is important to YOU on the map

Mapping Matters © Al Cane

CAN U DIG IT?
COME TO GARDENING CLUB
WEDNESDAYS 4-
less cars and pollution
green spaces
multicultural east oxford
This shows the main forces of change in our society, some already happening and some predicted to happen. They show what influences the issues and priorities you identified and stimulate discussion.
FORCES
SUPPORT LOCAL BUSINESSES
Is Internet shopping bad news for local business in East Oxford?
People want the diversity of local shops and business.
How do we encourage people to use them?
Should local shops and business provide locally sourced products?
What are the effects of multi-nationals on small business in East Oxford?
People are changing their consumption patterns, hi tech equipment like TV's and mobile phones
Increasing power of multinational companies
People are beginning to work from home more
More IT, Internet, virtual shopping
Out of town shopping centres are challenging city centres
People live away from where they work and commute more
People are taking more active roles in their communities
Local decisions are required to be made with more community involvement
People are more concerned and assertive about issues. They have less confidence in authorities to sort things out.
PROTECT GREEN SPACES FROM DEVELOPMENT
PROSECUTE POLLUTERS PROTECT TREES
What are the environmental threats to East Oxford?
What are the effects of climate change and pollution in the area?
How can green space be protected from development and affordable housing be provided.
Do developers have more influence than environmental groups?
How should pollution be monitored?
Climate change is beginning to have effects
More polluting substances and environmental destruction but also better laws to deal with pollution
Predictions of drought in UK, but also bouts of excessive rain leading to floods
Wildlife habitats and diversity are threatened

affordable housing
activities for young people
local businesses
CHANGE
People are more familiar with different cultures
Quality of life is a concern more so than just being well off
Increasing contact between different cultures and countries
More women are employed now, usually part time
BETTER THINGS FOR YOUNG PEOPLE TO DO
What facilities will suit the children of today?
How are children's expectations changing?
Do we need more facilities for the children of working parents?
How can facilities be shared between different cultures and generations?
Working hours and stress at work are increasing
There is an increase in the poverty gap and inequalities in health
GOOD MENTAL HEALTH CARE
Who are the vulnerable people and what support do they need?
The houses we live in are getting older and deteriorating
mental health facilities
cycling and safety

Mapping Matters © Al Cane

Home-Start Oxford

By Rosalind Lacey

with thanks to the Revd Barbara Hayes, Oxford Industrial Chaplaincy, and Tan Lea, Director of Sure Start, Rose Hill – Littlemore

First impressions of Oxford are of a city often teeming with young people, many of them students from the two universities; of beautiful buildings and historic monuments; of a centre of culture, learning and scholarship where in the past turbulent parts of our history have been enacted. But there is another side of Oxford – a side that not so many see, apart from the homeless in the central area, one of poverty and deprivation, of lack of opportunity and poor facilities.

A vision for the future of Oxford must be inclusive and involve those from the outer housing estates as well as those living in leafier parts. If the vision includes quality of life then much needs to be done to improve facilities in particular neighbourhoods.

In the recently published Government Index of Multiple Deprivation (IMB), wards in Oxford, notably Blackbird Leys, Littlemore and Temple Cowley, are nationally among 20% of those with low incomes. In what is described as the "education domain", these areas are in the worst 10% nationally.

On the positive side there are many voluntary organisations in Oxford working towards helping different groups in our society including Asylum Welcome, Age Concern, Archway, Gateway, Samaritans. These charities offer a huge number of opportunities to those who want to volunteer, which says a great deal about our sense of community, but we still need more who are willing to give time.

I am writing about one such organisation, Home-Start Oxford, a voluntary body in which volunteers offer regular support, friendship and practical help to families with at least one child under five, at times of stress. This support is provided in the family's own home, helping to prevent crisis and encouraging parents to cope with their problems and make better use of other resources available in the community.

Home-Start Oxford is one of over 300 schemes in the UK. For 14 years it has served the city of Oxford. In 2001-2, over 101 families were supported by 59 volunteers who visit once or twice a week. Families are referred by health visitors, social workers, GPs and others. Families can also refer themselves.

It is difficult to quantify the difference a Home-Start volunteer can make to a family, but, based on referrers' comments and on visits made by the Home-Start co-ordinator to the families concerned, from our monitoring and evaluation it can be proved that the benefits are measurable. Fewer children are taken into care; parents who have moved to Oxford feel less isolated; mothers with a child with disabilities are encouraged to make use of the facilities provided in the community; volunteers encourage families to keep appointments, with the school, the doctor, the hospital and often accompany them.

Over the past two years, Home-Start has also been involved with the Sure Start project in Rose Hill - Littlemore. Sure Start is a government initiative aimed at reducing social exclusion in disadvantaged areas by making an impact on children's health, their social and emotional development and their ability to learn.

Funding is provided to strengthen families and communities, to promote a community-based approach and to develop preventative services. There are now many Sure Start projects in the UK, but the Rose Hill - Littlemore scheme was one of the first. Home-Start Oxford provides support for an extra 20 families in this area, liaising closely with others in the Sure Start team.

Both Home-Start and Sure Start have visions for the future based on the different types of preventative work they do with young families in breaking the cycle of deprivation and offering opportunities for dealing with problems as they arise. Young parents may be experiencing isolation, suffering from post-natal depression or other mental illness, caring for a disabled child or are disabled themselves. They may be refugees or living in bed and breakfast accommodation. When they can be given support by a volunteer befriender on a regular basis, they can be helped to cope with their difficulties and problems. Often they can surmount these so that their children benefit from a less stressful environment, both in terms of health and in their response to education.

However, visions do not come free; in this real world, visions require financing. My personal vision would include a realisation that to create a more equitable society extra funding has to be found for voluntary organisations, including Home-Start Oxford, where the number of families supported is directly related to the number of co-ordinator hours we can afford. Core funders are the Early Years and Child Care Services, which are part of Oxfordshire County Council Education Service, and Sure Start. More money would mean that Home-Start could expand the service it is presently offering to the community. More families would then benefit from help at a critical time. The knock-on effect on the children would be of great significance and local communities on the outskirts of Oxford would be strengthened.

If we help future citizens of Oxford to feel they belong to a community then this vision for Oxford will be a shared one, for all the people.

Focus on the Earliest Years:
The Oxford Parent Infant Project

By Anna Murray

OXPIP's premise: there is increasing proof that the first two years of life are the most crucial for healthy emotional development. Neglectful or abusive treatment of infants will cause, in many cases, predictable problems for the child, the family and society at large. Early intervention can be effective. OXPIP, a charity started in 1998, supports parents with babies under 2 in developing secure relationships together through weekly sessions with experienced, friendly counsellors. Parents are asked to make an affordable contribution to the service.

OXPIP is based at the Healthy Living Centre in Temple Cowley; its counsellors also work at Sure Start in Rose Hill and Littlemore, at Blackbird Leys. The first mother-baby group has just begun. OXPIP also runs training workshops and information sessions for other professionals. It has applied to the Community Fund for money for a Randomised Control Trial which will measure the service's effectiveness. The OXPIP vision: to develop a model of a countywide, locally based service which could then be replicated nationally. As Ros Lacey says above,'visions require financing'. Our three year grant from the Community Fund expires in December, 2004. It is vital that there be extra funding for OXPIP (and Oxford's other voluntary organisations). We urgently need interested people to become Friends of OXPIP.

Helen Ganly, the first Artist in Residence at the Ashmolean Museum, has generously created inspiring drawings, such as the ones reproduced here, for OXPIP.

Living in Blackbird Leys

Kate Miller interviews Cora Spencer, 23/01/2002

Cora Spencer welcomed us into her home where she and her family have lived for almost forty years. She is a dynamic and inspiring person, who has been active in an impressive list of Oxford organisations. She has seen some big changes from the early days of Blackbird Leys, but she still loves living there.

At first there were animals next door on farmland and although it was originally planned to leave the site open, ideas changed and Windale First School was built there. A community farm shop was also planned for the site but instead, in a converted barn, the Pathfinder Workshops were developed. These are a vital part of the community, providing training in crafts for adults with disabilities. The building is also well-used for activities such as weddings and is the home of the Blackbird Bonanza, a lottery which provides funds for computers and other equipment for communal use or gives grants to needy individuals.

The Holy Family Church, a spacious, modern building with several generous community buildings, is central to a strong spirit of togetherness and caring. Many different projects, for example the credit union and the advice centre, were initiated and are run by a team of members of the congregation. They use church premises and are helped by the hard work of the vicar, James Ramsay, his colleague Fleur Houston and Jim Hewitt, the church community worker. The church is well supported by the residents and it is encouraging that many families who do not regularly attend church are keen to have their babies baptised. Greater Leys, the newest part of the estate, is becoming quite well integrated with the rest; Fleur Houston and her family live there.

One of Cora's ideals is for the outside world not to judge Blackbird Leys by adverse publicity, but instead to come to see and learn the actuality of the many good things that go on. The feeling of caring and personal knowledge of each other is much better than the public perception despite the population being about 13,500. She herself, having lived here for so long, has many friends and knows most families and their youngsters. She generates and gives much respect and she exerts a firm influence towards good behaviour. She became very angry and frustrated during the unpleasant period about nine years ago when stolen cars were raced around the roads of the estate.

Her sister living in New York telephoned Cora in consternation to ask if she and her family were safe, to receive Cora's brisk reply that she had just walked calmly over from the church and there was nothing going on at all. Of course the joy-riding was tiresome and dangerous, but in the end it was short-lived. In Cora's opinion it was much exaggerated by the media, whose negative international publicity created a stigma on the image of Blackbird Leys which was quite unfair and which unfortunately still lingers.

Cora's hope for the future of Blackbird Leys is that it should not lose its tradition of togetherness, but that this should continue and be strengthened and indeed be seen as an example for the wider area.

Part II

•••••

Designing a Better City

Courtesy Roger Evans Urban Design Strategy

Young Ideas

By Emily Brown and Class 8, 2002
Frideswide Middle School

My vision for Oxford would be to develop the city for the young people. Simply offering more activities for the young would make Oxford a better place to live. Having a good sized swimming pool, with reasonable prices, is, in my opinion, a necessity within the city. Improved sporting facilities would be an asset to the centre of Oxford, at prices which everyone can afford, rather than overpriced members-only sports clubs.

Not only should there be more things to do in Oxford, there should be safe ways to access these facilities: safer cycle routes that you can cycle in and feel comfortable should be a priority. These cycle routes should not mean having to cycle around the buses when they are stopped at bus stops and going into the busy and dangerous traffic. This is not just for young cyclists, for all cyclists in Oxford would benefit from improved safety and it would make cycling more popular, which in turn would reduce the quantity of traffic and improve the appearance and air quality of the city.

The wooded areas around the city must remain intact; the green belts must not be built on. The parks are vital for families, dog owners and for everyone in the community. It would be awful to see Oxford in ten years with no grassed areas, just full of housing.

Oxford is a beautiful city, for all who live there and for all who visit each year. My vision for Oxford is that it retains its famous attractions; the Cherwell river, the parks, the buildings and the dreaming spires, but that the city adapts to the twenty first century. It should be made safer, have more facilities for the young, but still attract tourists for years to come rather than becoming known for its traffic, pollution, poor facilities and lack of green spaces.

Emily

Oxford-on-Sea

Oxford City in 2012
Could be a little haven
From the ever advancing threat
Of Technology.

In picuresque little side streets
We sit at pavement cafes.
We enjoy the recent Climate
Change and a cooling
Breeze from the always encroaching
Warm waters of the Channel.
A newly created beach where
People are relaxed.

Oxford City in 2012
Could be a little haven
From the ever advancing threat
Of Technology.

Mira

I would like Oxford to be a safe place, where mothers don't have to worry whether their children will be safe when they play outside; where old ladies don't feel threatened walking down alley- ways late at night.

I would like Oxford to be a happy place, where there aren't any homeless people; where everyone is smiling.

Isla

lots more trees

Oxford in 10 years
No homeless people
Everyone to be rich
A house made of chocolate
Flying cars
Less traffic
Biggest free shopping mall in the world
Able to drive when you're 10 or over
Stricter laws on gangs
No smoking, no drug taking
Death sentences for paedophiles
No school uniforms
More hospitals
Superman
Bigger cinemas
More advanced cinemas
Rain made out of money
More rights for kids
No greedy people
NO WEAPONS AND WAR
A gingerbread mansion
Everyone respecting each other and
everyone around them and nature.
Everyone to care for animals.

Merlin

bicycle taxis
a train that runs through the city centre.
An 'Oxford eye'
mini's
no big cars
mini metro

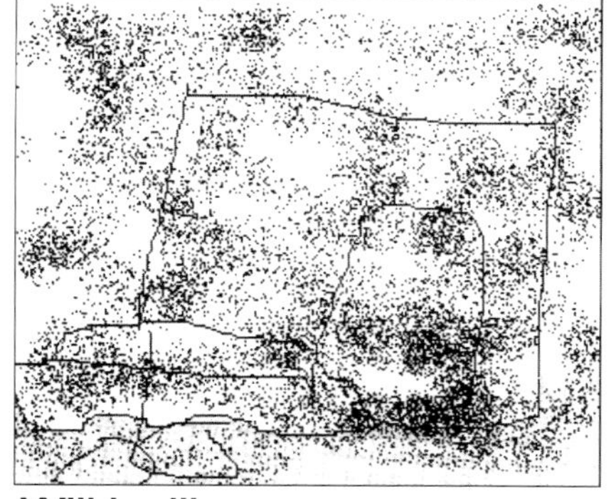

Will be like
by Katherine

This is a picture of pollution in Oxford. I have drawn a picture of a car to symbolize the over use of objects that produce harmful gases and fumes. I have also drawn a picture of a shop to symbolize the growing amount of shops. *Katherine*

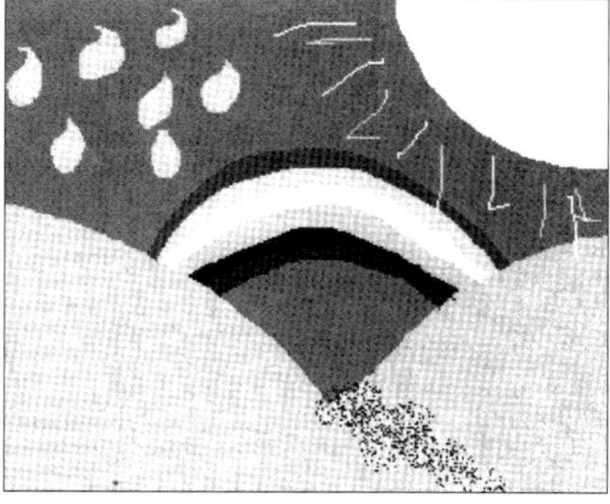

Should be Like
by Grace

I have drawn a picture of hills to show that land should be left as it is and not built on. I think that there are too many big factories and cars so I have chosen to draw a scene without these. I have also drawn a rainbow because they are my favourite things and make me think of happiness. I have also drawn a stream this is because they are nice natural things. *Grace*

crudity faintly suggestive of human sacrifice and yet miserably skimpy.

Said Business School, Oxford
Photo Edmund Gray

Wherever hills provide opportunity, housing should be ranged in tiers to maximise the view, with an increase in height from tier to tier if necessary. Anyone inclined to react against such a layout should consider Bath or any Italian hill city. It should be added that building at greater density and greater heights is entirely compatible with considerable tree planting, even on balconies and roofs. This would allow some of the higher building to blend into the landscape, as would the use of brick, rather than the staring white surface of the John Radcliffe Hospital, whose bulky outline is indeed no enhancement of the scene.

The need for greater density is not the only reason for rebuilding much of Oxford, especially the inner residential areas that were put up between the tail end of the nineteenth century and 1914. One good reason is the poor aesthetic quality, for even those houses of slightly more pretension reach no higher than speculative builders' red brick "Queen Anne". Most are in terraces, some in semi-detached pairs, but they lack any unifying coherence of design, indeed not infrequently consist of a jumble of discordant groups. They are laid out in streets that are over-long or straggle in unconsidered curves, with no regard for scenic effect or variety. There are almost no squares, crescents or other interesting layouts, and no focal points in the form of public buildings or churches, which are simply fitted in between the houses.

Secondly, they are nearly all ill-planned for modern life, having rather small rooms, obstructive chimney breasts and constricting rear wings. Quite a number are tiny. Wholesale rebuilding would be more economical and give better results than a multitude of individual loft conversions, extensions and wall-removals. It would also remedy the absence of garages, which means that cars have to stand in ugly rows along the pavements, and the roadways are often too narrow either for two-way traffic or for the taller houses that I believe are necessary.

The difficulty in the way of wholesale rebuilding to a much improved layout is that there is virtually no way of achieving it under present planning arrangements. Local authorities have powers of compulsory purchase, but their use for comprehensive re-building is so fraught with difficulties and expense that they are rarely, if ever, used and private developers could never hope to accumulate the freeholds of the necessary number of adjoining houses, which is one reason they are always after green-field sites. What is needed is a new form of the method by which Nash cleared away a whole swathe of run-down Westminster and rebuilt everything to a fresh street layout from the Mall to Regents Park. He and his colleagues specified the external design of the buildings that were put up by builders who took long leases on the sites. There was therefore public control over planning and design, but private financing of most of the cost.

To enable such a process to be replicated, legislation should give local authorities the power to buy compulsorily at market prices all the properties within an area designated as in need of improvement. They should set the layout and design in the public interest and lease or sell the component units of construction to developers who could be free to design the interiors or other subordinate aspects in co-ordination with the overall architects to achieve an integrated result. A rolling programme of construction and demolition could allow occupants being bought out the option of transferring to homes in the immediate vicinity. Leasehold tenure or a management covenant could serve to maintain the initial unity of design into the future, including external colour where appropriate.

The great rebuilding that I am proposing will inevitably be a slow process. The first area to be taken in hand ought, I suggest, to be East Oxford, either side of the Cowley Road. It is worth noting that Cowley Road itself is so down-at-heel that few probably notice that it has a curve with as much picturesque potential as High Street - and even now offers a fine vista of St Mary's, ready to be framed by handsome terraces, a tower or two and other enlivening features such as miniature squares and arch-fronted pedestrian precincts, as well as benches and trees.

Although this is not the place for yet another deep analysis of Oxford traffic or detailed proposals for its handling, one cannot discuss the architectural fabric of the city, still less the rebuilding of whole areas, without at least some consideration of roads. There is now, I believe, general rejection of the policy of building roads until we have catered for all the traffic that may wish to use them. It is recognised that this would destroy the fabric of the city and civilised life within it. We have not, however, fully adjusted to the adoption of the alternative strategy of restricting traffic to the level that is compatible with a humane city. This implies, for instance, that dual carriageways built in the days of the old approach should be abolished. All streets should belong to pedestrians, either wholly or at least in equality with vehicles. There should be continuous frontages of shops, houses or other buildings to all streets except where there are parks or scenic open spaces, and streets should be aligned for the convenience and visual satisfaction of pedestrians rather than for the transit of vehicles. Shapeless curves and windy intersections designed for traffic should be eliminated.

New student accommodation for St John's College.
Photo Edmund Gray

However, the rejection of road schemes dedicated to traffic should not mean that no road improvements at all should take place. In principle, if traffic is held at low volume, modest speed and undisturbing noise level by parking restrictions, road pricing and the like, what there is of it should be allowed to circulate freely. And if streets are never subordinated to vehicles, there is every reason for providing an even network of them throughout built-up areas and the traffic correspondingly dispersed - with due allowance for pedestrian precincts, historic buildings and other valuable features. One-way improvisations should be done away with and bottlenecks minimised. The policy of channelling traffic along a few main roads and inhibiting it elsewhere, which is a hangover from the days of trying to provide for as much traffic as possible, moving as speedily as possible, should be abandoned. It is bad for the humane quality of the main roads, and forces what traffic there is into unnecessarily circuitous routes.

In Oxford terms, all these considerations imply, above all, the rebuilding of St Ebbe's without the main dual carriageway or its car-dominated branches or many of its very ungracious recent buildings. There should instead be a network of streets planned to offer visual delights drawn from the repertory of past centuries but meeting the practicalities of today - such as avenues closed by tall, eye-catching buildings, sudden openings of narrow streets to open squares, geometric quarter-curves or sequences of straight blocks angled to one another, with vertical features at salient angles. Such devices do not stale like the borrowings from past styles of facade. Similarly, we should learn from Venice and Amsterdam how to make the stretch of the Thames through St Ebbe's glorious with tall and stately buildings. And why not include the unexecuted design for a house in the Grand Canal by Frank Lloyd Wright, one of the greatest of architects, who was never invited to work in Britain? At the moment, the 1970s terraces try to look lower than they are in an apology for existing, with the top floors usually in the roof slope, giving a blind look from outside and denying a view of the river from the inside. Is it possible to have a more negative attitude to a marvellous site?

An imaginative bridge across the Thames from St Ebbe's could both enhance the river and form an alternative route westwards to that of Park End Street and Botley Road. Instead of the depressing sump under the railway between these two streets, people on foot as well as in vehicles could traverse an avenue through St Ebbe's terminating at the far end of the bridge in a dramatic building, like the College de France in Paris or the Castel S Angelo in Rome. The much needed concert hall could fulfil this role. And the bridge could be lined with statues like the Ponte S Angelo or the Charles Bridge in Prague. The road could perhaps split around the concert hall, one branch going southwards parallel to Abingdon Road, the other broadly parallel to Botley Road, utilising Osney Mead as its first stretch.

To the north of St Ebbe's the streets around the castle should be re-aligned to make more of it as a focal point. The Castle Mound to my eyes also suffers from the lack of anything on its summit, once crowned by a Norman keep. It would obviously be wrong to attempt to replace this with any kind of building, but I suggest the erection of something in the way of a large-scale sculpture - perhaps the Monument to the Unknown Political Prisoner by Reg Butler, designed to be placed on the white cliffs of Dover but never erected for political reasons. This may shock people who like things as they are; yet the same people would probably be insistent on the retention of a summit monument if it had been there for a century or two.

The castle area should also be improved by removing the worst eyesore of central Oxford, the Worcester Street car park. There should instead be a garden bordering the Castle Stream, perhaps flanked by small buildings shielding it from the traffic. Apart from other merits, this would terminate the vista down the quadrangle of Nuffield College and through its western archway.
Further west, the space between Park End Street and the Said Business School is of the rectangular shape that fits it to become one of Oxford's few squares, instead of being an over-complicated traffic junction. If the seventeenth-century Carfax Conduit, removed to Nuneham Park in 1787, were re-erected in the centre, it

would provide a focus for the square and a foil for the Business School, mitigating the rather hard look of its void-and-flush-surface style, which is at least preferable to the jagged, falling-over look, the other main Post-Modernist style.

There is a good case for more sculpture throughout the city. We should emulate the Germans, who fill their cities with fountains, sculptures and ironwork decoration, much of it figurative: imbued with flair, imagination and wit – and rarely vulgar as figurative sculpture tends to be in Britain - where the alternative goes to the opposite extreme: exploring the limits of avant-gardism by artists bent on "challenging" and "disturbing" the onlooker rather than embellishing the streets, as if we did not have rather too much to disturb us already. Sculptures of the right kind can be appreciated by all kinds of people including children, for whom some can provide climbing adventures. It would also be good to see some more interesting iron work, in the way of gates, grilles, signs and the like. And the city council should also persist with the traditional cast iron street names and abandon the blander, less impressive plastic substitutes.

The Carfax Conduit
Photo David Clark

Turning northwards in the consideration of the street system, it would be in line with the general principles I have suggested that Walton Street should share some of the traffic now using Woodstock Road and that the very narrow Hayfield Road (its northward continuation) should be rebuilt to a more reasonable scale - highly desirable anyhow, as the houses are tiny and far from beautiful.

On the east side of Summertown, Charlbury Road could be extended northwards as far as Cutteslowe. This would give the opportunity for a series of fine terraces with an outlook on the Cherwell meadows. These terraces and their counterparts elsewhere on the edge of built-up areas could either form a picturesque backdrop to the surrounding meadows, as Merton and Christ Church do to Christ Church Meadow, or look out on a woodland screen.

In East Oxford, there should be a number of cross-routes and in particular one forming something approaching a straight line from Donnington Bridge to Headington, replacing the present routes which are both very roundabout and too narrow for the comfort of residents and drivers.

Additional river crossings should not be excluded from consideration, provided they are designed so as to intrude only minimally on the flood meadows which they cross and provided they are offset by enlargements or improvements to meadowland or waterways elsewhere. There is, for instance, a case for the often-proposed Thames crossing via Eastwyke Farm and Jackdaw Lane. Why shouldn't such a bridge be an adornment to the scene, like Magdalen Bridge, rather than bleakly utilitarian like those of the 1950s?

So habituated have we become to all road "improvements" being dedicated solely to the convenience of traffic that I must stress again that I am only proposing new streets and bridges so designed to be pleasing to residents and pedestrians at least as much as convenient to drivers. This does not require an attitude of blanket hostility to cars, an attitude that seems to be gaining ground, in spite of the fact that most people use cars habitually - and there is no prospect of cars disappearing. Some of the traffic lights in Oxford and some of the road humps and pinches seem designed out of malice rather than out of calculation of net benefit to all road users. Those who devise them also ignore cycles, buses and taxis, although the use of these is supposed to be encouraged. It should not be necessary to point out that to avoid impeding cycles, there should always be gaps in humps for them to pass through and pinches should never be so narrow as to force cycles to give way to oncoming vehicles. As for the wedge-sided humps of some Oxford streets, which reduce cars to about 1mph, they constitute gross obstacles to bicycles, imposing both discomfort and delay – to say nothing of the effect on ambulances hurrying to hospitals with patients for whom jolts may be dangerous as well as excruciating. They should be removed forthwith.

Cyclists are ostensibly favoured in Oxford, but their interests are often not met. Some roads are decidedly uneven or damaged and the Oxford Transport Strategy introduced features markedly hostile to cycles - notoriously the cobbled surface in Park End Street but also the proliferation of traffic lights on the approach to the station, which have the absurd affect of making it generally quicker to get off and wheel a cycle. Some bus routes are similarly afflicted.

Blinking amber traffic lights, widespread on the Continent to indicate permission to advance cautiously, and familiar here on pedestrian lights, should be adopted in this country. They would benefit all traffic at certain roundabouts and other intersections during off-peak hours, but would be particularly applicable to cyclists at some types of junction, especially for those riding due ahead at T-junctions permitting them to share the road with pedestrians though yielding priority to them, as happens already where pedestrians cheerfully stray on to the roadway in the Turl, George Street and elsewhere, without ill consequences. A tougher line could then be taken with cyclists jumping red lights. In the same spirit, the use by cyclists of many of the bridleways and footbridges in Oxford, which is well established in practice and unofficially tolerated, should be facilitated by the lowering of kerbs and the modification of barriers.

All these measures would do more to encourage people to take to cycles than the laying of unsightly green strips along main roads and the accompanying multiplication of signs, occasionally half a dozen thick - as if those erecting them were oblivious either of the need to save money or the desirability of curbing visual clutter.

For the pedestrian, Oxford offers a wealth of paths - more than most people are aware of, but there is a lack of through routes, apart from the towpaths. They should be matched by paths traversing the full length of the green wedges that reach into the centre of Oxford. One along the Cherwell serves as prime example. At present, a series of gaps and obstacles blocks its route. It could begin with an elegant bridge over the Thames at the confluence of the two rivers, linking the towpath with Christ Church Meadow. Via Rose Lane and the open garden in front of the Botanic Garden, it could perhaps use the existing passage under Magdalen Bridge and the slipway by Magdalen Tower to reach the far pavement of the bridge. From the middle of the bridge, steps could lead down to Greyhound Meadow. At the north end of the meadow, there could be another interesting bridge, leaping across both the western arm of the Cherwell (divided at this point) and the narrow strip of Magdalen Fellows' Garden bordering the river. Virtue could be made of the necessary span of this bridge by crowning it with a decorative balustrade and a belvedere in spiky wood, which would ornament the scene and offer a view of the spires of Oxford from an unusual angle. The bridge would debouch on the path along the west bank of the Cherwell which forms a spur of the University Parks. Midway along the eastern border of the Parks there is already a footbridge leading to a path extending

The west bank of the Cherwell.
Photo Edmund Gray

northwards along the east bank of the Cherwell to Marston Ferry Road and beyond. Access to this path from Summertown across the meadows could be served by two or three new footbridges.

The inhabitants of Summertown can at present reach the Cherwell only by walking most of the way down the cheerless Marston Ferry Road. Similarly there is a lack of (legitimate) paths from Summertown to the Oxford Canal and beyond it, across the railway, to Port Meadow. At least one proper path should be opened.

There is a crying need for a comprehensive map of Oxford paths. Maintenance of the paths and their surroundings should be improved too, with more people doing this work and fewer sitting behind desks. Many of the existing and proposed paths could also be enhanced by tree planting, screening the less picturesque buildings and especially reducing the impact of the bypass, both visually and in terms of noise. In many places, some quite close to the centre of Oxford, it is possible to imagine one is in deep country. That magic could be extended at relatively low cost by skilful planting – with more benefit, in my view, than the tree planting that is sometimes suggested for the historic centre of the city, where it would tend to obstruct the view of the architecture.

The bypass should be as little of a barrier as possible to the paths that cross it. Broad underpasses, approached through groves and having the air of grottoes, might be one jolly way of doing this; another might be bridges wide enough to enclose the walker in vegetation or at least a creeper-clad pergola. The noise of the bypass is another of its disagreeable features, from which many parts of Oxford suffer badly. It should be reduced in every way possible, especially by low-noise asphalt but also by earthbanks or cuttings.

Noise in towns is a subject that does not get enough attention. The sirens of emergency vehicles are hideously loud in Oxford, almost certainly of a level damaging to hearing. They should be replaced by quieter, more euphonious signals that are easier to locate, and if that slows them, which I do not believe, money should be found to speed the process of dealing with emergencies in other ways to compensate. It is a sign of modern barbarism that we tolerate this odious feature of life, which contrasts so painfully with the magical sound of clock chimes and bells dominant not so long ago.

This contribution has been mainly about architecture and planning, but the vision I have proposed intermeshes with a more general vision. As technology advances, unskilled, disagreeable and monotonous work should melt away and we can envisage a more equal society, in which economic growth, driven by the desire to catch up with other peoples' wealth, can yield place to the higher goals of building civilisation and living in harmony. Equality means greater community of culture and outlook, with clear benefits for the well-being of cities. Crime can be expected to fall, the run-down and sub-standard areas of the less well-off can at last disappear and the clashes of taste of different economic groups can vanish. To achieve this happy state, we must think positively to channel the forces of history in the right direction, rather than merely trying to hold back the tide of changes we do not like – just as I suggest we do in the more specific fields of architecture and planning.

A Civilised City Quarter

By Roger Evans

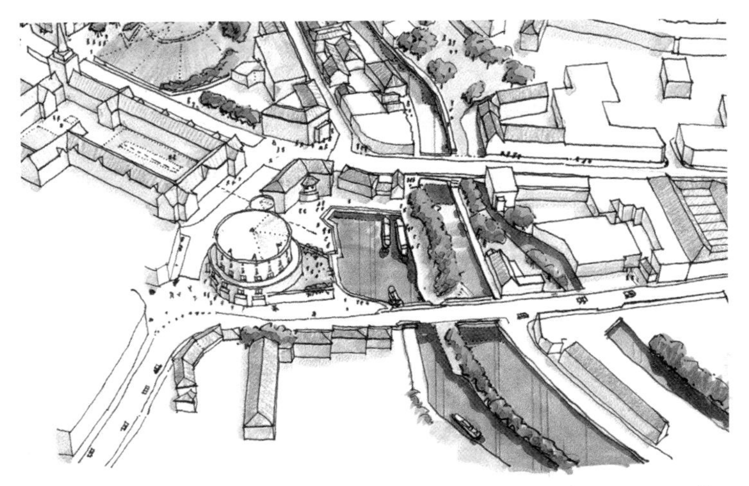

Birdseye view over Hythe Bridge street with proposed Concert Hall and reinstated canal basin. Courtesy Roger Evans Associates

All cities have been designed, whether it is the thousand cumulative small decisions made by the burghers of the medieval city or the Renaissance master plan formally setting out axes and vistas, they are all planned. Until relatively recently in mankind's history, the backbone around which towns and cities were made was within the public realm, the network of streets, squares and parkland from which we experience our built environment. Historically, cities grew along public spaces. Society is supported, and common values established, in part through the shared use of public spaces. Quite simply, when everyone turns their house to face and form a street or public space, they are, by that act, valuing community; they are making an investment in that space. It is through contact with others that individuals become a community and society is formed. That network of public space provides a common ground, in both a geographical and spiritual sense. In the medieval city, almost all buildings were at least in part residential and the street accommodated trade and provided outdoor meeting rooms. For the Renaissance city, the major streets also performed a ceremonial function and provided a higher order of spatial structure; for Haussmann's Paris, it provided boulevards that traversed the warren of medieval streets, convenient for policing but also assisting orientation and the movement of horse drawn carriages.

Such an understanding of the role of the public realm was largely forgotten from the middle of the twentieth century. Streets became conduits for motorcars rather than social places for people on foot. New developments were built on campus sites, inward - looking rather than addressing the street, and occupants were expected to drive between developments. As the urban theorist Kevin Lynch pointed out, "the traditional street served many functions beyond that of passage. It was a market, a workroom and a meeting hall. We have shouldered these functions out of the 'right-of-way' to the advantage of traffic and to society's loss".

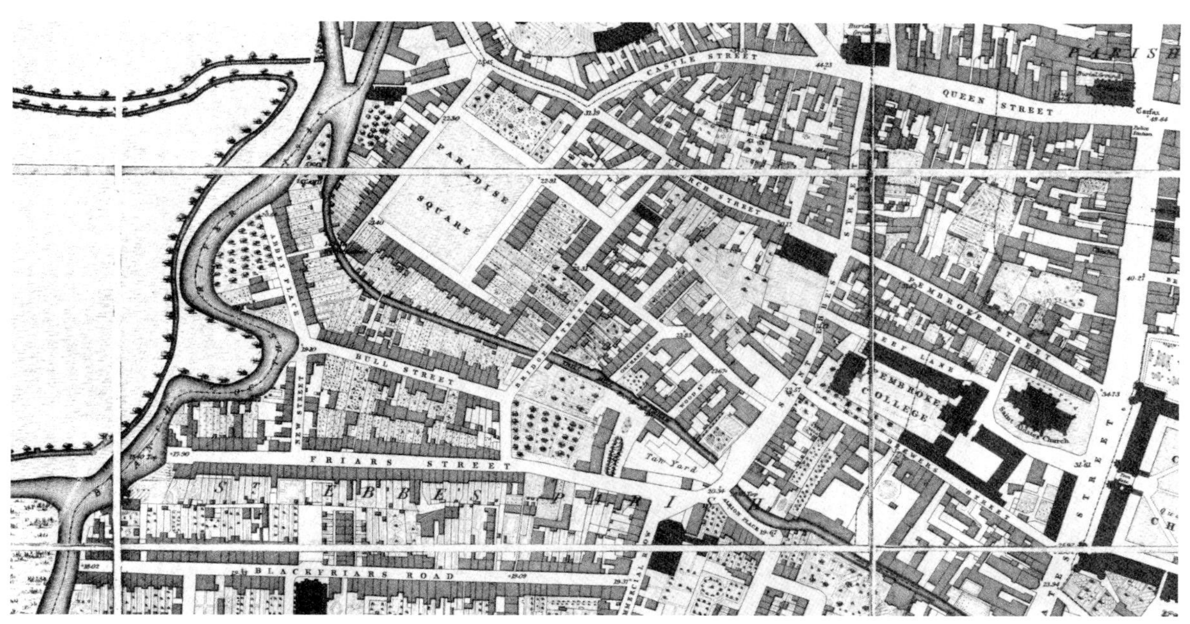

Part of Hoggar's Map of Oxford (Carfax at top right)
© Oxfordshire County Council Photographic Archive

If we look at Hoggar's map of Oxford in 1850 we see a spatial pattern that has some key characteristics in common with all cherished cities. **Figure 1** (p.98) redraws Hoggar's map to show buildings, private spaces and the public realm. We can observe a lattice structure of connected streets; a fine grain to the street pattern, with streets between 60 and 120 metres apart; a clear spatial hierarchy where the more important streets are either wider or have a greater containment afforded by taller buildings; buildings that addressed the street from which they gained access and provided informal surveillance and security. The street plan is legible. It would be possible for a visitor to parachute in without a street map and instinctively find his way to the centre of the city or around the various city quarters and have a shrewd idea of where the principal public buildings would be located and what might be found along the back lanes.

Have our needs for a safe, convenient, legible and social city plan changed over the last few decades? We are still born with two legs, walk at about 5 kph, are prepared to take a five minute walk for routine tasks. That characteristic still defines the size of a neighbourhood. If public space is to facilitate human contact, then scale is critical. At 150 metres we can discern body gestures, at 25 metres we can recognise a friend's face, at 12 metres make out facial expressions and at six metres the subtleties of speech and gesture can be conveyed. Such human characteristics which determined the shape and form of our city habitats have been increasingly ignored. The popular travel writer Bill Bryson notes that "architects and city planners and everyone else responsible for urban life seem to have lost sight of what cities are for. They are for people. That seems obvious enough, but for over half a century we have been building cities that are for almost anything else: for cars, for businesses, for developers, for people with money and bold visions who refuse to see cities from ground level, as places in which people must live and function and get around. Why should I have to walk through a damp tunnel and negotiate two sets of stairs to get across a busy street? Why should cars be given priority over us? How can we be so rich and stupid at the same time? We used to build civilisations. Now we build shopping malls."

Fig. 1. Oxford past
(derived from Hoggar's map 1850).

Fig. 2. Oxford today.

Fig. 3. Oxford future

No, our needs have not changed, but the process of planning our cities has changed in two important respects. First, we often fail to take an overview of the kind of places that we are creating. The emergence of separate professional disciplines has led to buildings, roads and landscape often being designed in isolation from each other with a resultant confusion. Secondly, we have lost our nerve to plan cities; we have become reactive rather than pro-active. We respond to planning applications by seeking to negotiate details of the scheme; we are reticent to set out clear plans for what is required in an area in anything other than in the most general terms and for relatively small areas for fear of frightening away developers. The result can be seen in **figure 2.** Recently redeveloped parts of the city are confused and confusing; the public realm has no comprehensible or convenient pattern. Pedestrian space, and the informal social contact that it facilitates, has been lost to traffic corridors. A convergence of interests in recent decades has led to large scale redevelopments where public streets are replaced by indoor centres. Investors get a large, uncomplicated addition to a property portfolio, developers a substantial property deal and local authorities a means of attracting development with the minimum of effort.

Developers however like certainty above all else, both in terms of what is permissible on a given site and also in what is going to happen in the surrounding area. The line that it is 'not possible to set out street patterns in advance of knowing developers requirements' is mistaken. Traditional city blocks can accommodate any use appropriate to a city centre, although many developers like to convert public streets into private malls and so control the behaviour of potential customers. The notion that we just respond to development pressures by processing planning applications is an abdication of responsibilities. It is a political issue; are we promoting a city which can be used by all our citizens and visitors or are we solely engaged in a series of property deals? But even property deals carried out in the absence of an adequate master plan for the city quarter cannot achieve the best result for the public purse. There is not a conflict between a well designed city quarter and land values, indeed, the long term success of a plan can be judged by the long-term land values created for the wider area. Places that are attractive to people will in turn attract investment.

In the south-west quarter of Oxford we have actually devalued land. The Inspector's report into the recent Oxpens Leisure Village Inquiry stated that Oxpens was an out-of-town site. In other words, planning policies in the latter part of the century managed to convert land within five minutes' walk of Carfax into a peripheral location by virtue of layout and design. Even more extraordinary is the fact that the city is a major landowner and potentially a chief beneficiary of well laid out new development.

At the time of writing, a Government Green Paper on the planning system proposes that master plans be drawn up for key areas of all towns and cities as part of public participation exercises. Government is again encouraging planning after a period during the eighties and nineties of laissez-faire that saw very large-scale development occur in many historic cities with little input from local councils. Working with a single developer is often an easy way out for an authority that may well have ownership of much of the required development land as well as control over existing streets. A more creative way forward would be for the local authority to set out a preferred street structure that defines a number of plots of different sizes which can be developed by a larger number of players. It places the local authority in control of creating the public realm, encourages diversity, mixed use and can still accommodate major development on the larger plots (or whole block) while ensuring that all buildings are integrated into the wider context of the city.

The new millennium is an opportune time for the city and its people to decide what kind of city centre they want, not only in terms of the policy principles set out in the local plan but also as a detailed, three dimensional city form that will accommodate and nourish a vibrant social, cultural and economic community.

So what would the key ingredients be for such a plan? I suggest that a requirement of any plan for what is being termed the 'west end', the south-west quarter, of the city embodies the following seven principles:

- A logical network of connected streets that join the major assets, both topographical and built;
- A fine grain of streets that will promote walking and cycling by virtue of their permeability;
- A clear hierarchy of streets and public spaces that will create diversity and aid orientation;
- Development that addresses the street, not turning its back to public life; active edges comprising shops, services and buildings with public access at street level;
- A mix of uses along every street so that all places will be populated throughout the working day and into the evening;
- Architecture that is designed to address and overlook the street, thus providing natural surveillance and self-policing;
- Architecture that is appropriate to the street on which it sits, in terms of scale and architectural language.

Figure 3 shows a possible pattern for the south-western quarter of the city. There are other options and I would not pretend that this is the only solution. The plan does however embody those characteristics that I believe to be essential to creating a true city quarter that can extend the qualities of the historic city.

As I have said elsewhere, there is rarely an ideal time to replan a city quarter and never a clean slate on which to start. There are always remnants from the past, mistakes that will have to stand, obligations and commitments entered into which will have to be honoured. This is as it should be. The most remarkable cities are the result of modifications and interventions over many centuries and constraints imposed by the past serve as a reminder of our own limited tenure. We need to work with the past and future generations as well as the present.

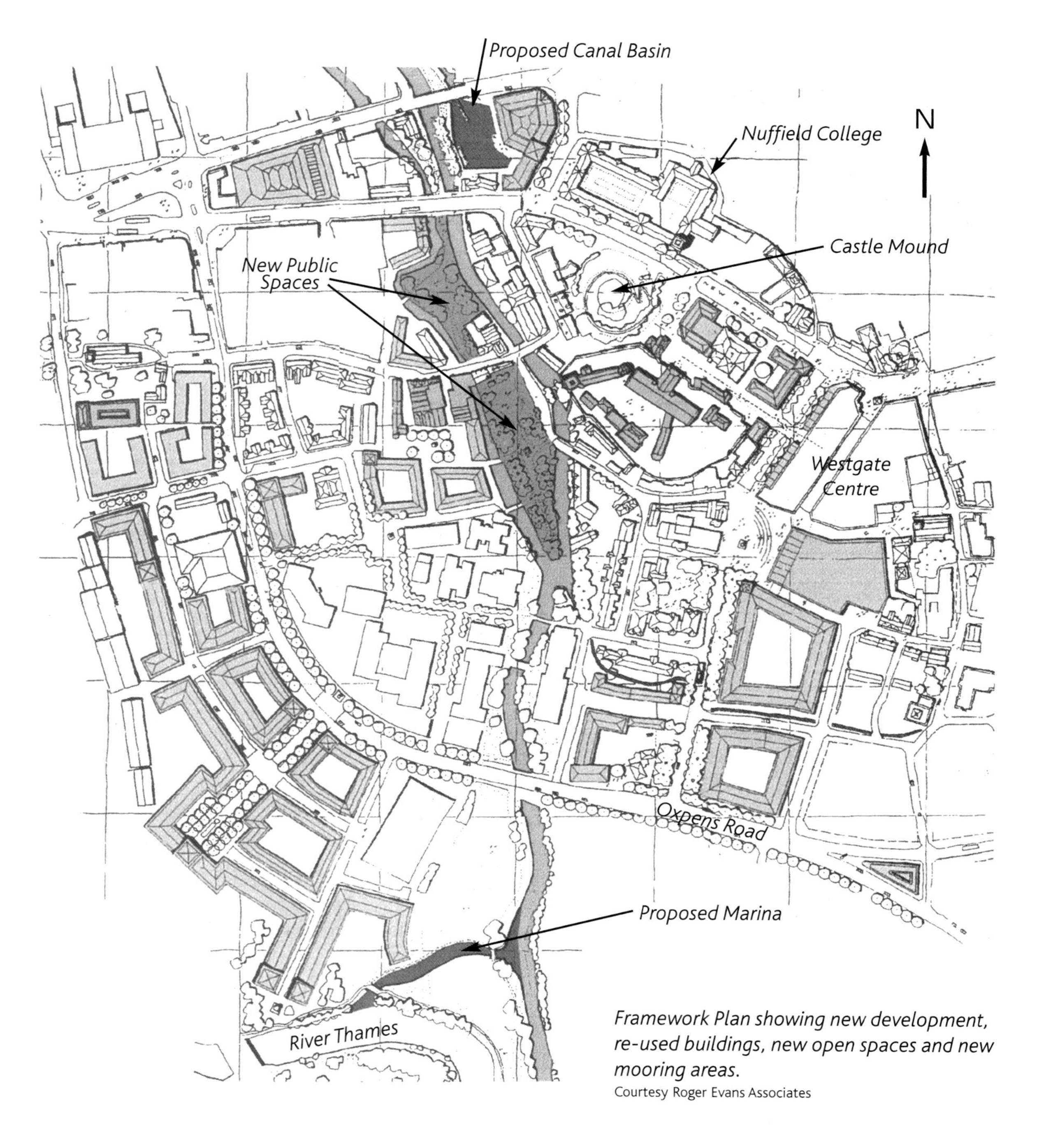

Framework Plan showing new development, re-used buildings, new open spaces and new mooring areas.
Courtesy Roger Evans Associates

The Castle Site

At last a vision becomes a reality

By Debbie Dance

As early as 1946 Oxford Preservation Trust minutes reveal concern over the fate of the Prison site with talk of the possibility of a public park and a museum. Fifty years later the Home Office eventually made up its mind and vacated the Prison and the County Council was able to acquire this extraordinary place, a hidden gem in the centre of the city and yet somehow outside it.

But what is this site that John Betjeman, then Trust Secretary, and others were so excited about? What lies behind the 19th century prison walls? What buildings? What history? What stories to tell? What has been revealed as we have researched, dug and delved, is a truly remarkable story. Layer upon layer of rich history have emerged, revealing the Saxon town, the dominance of the Normans who came and imposed their motte and bailey castle, of which only the Mound remains. The Church and College of St. George within the Castle - of which St. George's Tower and the Crypt remain, with their evidence of Geoffrey of Monmouth teaching here in the 1130s - mark the beginnings of the university. This is extraordinary stuff. A gaol in the castle is first mentioned in the 1230s and a prison remains here for over 750 years – this is serious history.

Add to this the medieval civil war conflicts between King Stephen and his cousin Empress Matilda, the romance and drama of her escape from the Castle one Christmas, slipping out in the snow, dressed all in white and accompanied by three knights – this is pure atmosphere.

Stories of the Black Assizes, of death and pestilence, Tudor poor laws and children imprisoned, of debtors and felons, punishment and suffering - there are so many stories to tell, and to tell on the very site, and within the very buildings, where they occurred. Executions, anatomy, transportation, prison reform and improvement all can be told through the written evidence of the very people who experienced them: witness the last public execution in 1863, the atmosphere of the huge crowd who gathered to witness, the coarse jests and ribald laughter followed by a painful and lasting silence.

But what of the vision for the future? Can we bring a new commercial life to this extraordinary site whilst keeping its character and atmosphere? The success will be to design a scheme which keeps the character of the site as a prison and as a castle and yet will invite people into it and not allow them to pass it by.

And what is planned within the walls? The main 19th century prison buildings, A Wing and C wing, are to be converted into a hotel with a difference. The stairs and gantries are to remain, the hotel rooms to be created within the cells, sometimes two or three together, but carefully done to maintain the cellular plan and repetitiveness which is so characteristic of the Blackburn "porridge" prison both inside and out. A new hotel building at the front, beside the Mound, has been designed by Dixon & Jones, the architects of Said Business School. Knocking down shops on Castle Street will open up this side of the site to the city, creating a new entrance to an area where shops and restaurants and a daily market will operate.

The Trust has never once wavered in its belief that its involvement would ensure public access and that the story of what is seen will be revealed for all. A successful bid to the Heritage Lottery Fund has allowed the creation of a Heritage Centre in the 18th century prison buildings of D Wing which joins the Debtors' Tower to St. Georges' Tower, with an access tunnel beneath into the 12th century Crypt. Taking down the 19th century prison wall will bring together the Tower and Castle Mound again, and enable the story of the earlier history of the site to be told. The wonderful space created with the backdrop of the Mound and Tower will be a new public square for the city, the Castleyard. A glass entrance to the new Heritage Centre at the base of the Tower will open on to the square as will the state-of-the-art Education Centre and the café allowing visitors to sit and watch the world go by.

The Heritage Centre is designed as an introduction to the history of the site, telling the story through the buildings and people within them. Audiotapes and guided tours will take you round the site to see and hear about A Wing, the Treadwheel House, the Punishment Cells and the Saxon Town Wall. Whether a casual visitor, local or international tourist, you will be able to take away something of what you see and be tempted to learn more. A viewing platform on St. George's Tower will look out across the site and the city, and there will be the chance to visit the atmospheric top floors of the Debtors' Tower, to climb the Mound and visit the Well Chamber.

In the day, city residents and visitors will be welcome to come and sit on the sympathetically designed permanent seating running along the base of the Mound, enjoy a drink or meal at the café or visit the Heritage Centre and its shop. Perhaps they will come to enjoy a traditional craft day with demonstrations and stalls, or to see the Morris dancers or other local events. In the evening, the seating will provide the chance for theatre performances and *son et lumière*.

What we will see is history in the making, a continuation of the site's 1000 years, a celebration of the clever and innovative way we re-use our heritage in the 21st century, a place for all to enjoy.

New Road hotel extension to prison building (architects Dixon & Jones) showing new walkway beside the Castle Mound with the Debtors Tower and St Goerge's Tower in the background.

A New Cultural Centre

By Alan Russell

There is a need for a concert hall/theatre/cultural centre on a site which could be readily accessible from east, west, north and south, which would enable buildings of real quality to be erected and give the city civic facilities in which residents of all parts of Oxford could take pride.

Fortunately, a superlative site exists at the foot of Jackdaw Lane, between Meadow Lane and the Thames – behind Christ Church Meadow. It is scandalous that this beautiful riverside land has been occupied for decades by an old car dump. Here is a site of ten acres or more which would be ample for a concert hall/theatre, a hotel, a car park connected by roads to Jackdaw Lane and to Donnington Bridge, and any other necessary supporting facilities. With careful tree planting, the whole ensemble could be made to enhance rather than diminish the much loved views down the river towards the old city centre.

Over time, it could become a key element in a corridor through the university and Christ Church sports grounds into St Clements, on to the Marston Road and through the Mesopotamia Walks to the University Parks. Especially if the Parks could be extended on to the eastern side of the Cherwell and linked by footpaths through the Walks and Angel Meadow to the Botanic Garden and Christ Church Meadow, then all Oxford residents would be able to feel that in the very heart of their city lay a band of university and civic facilities created for the benefit of all. This would in addition put Oxford even more firmly on the tourist map, without adding to the overcrowding of the medieval town.

A new, light and elegant bridge, for cyclists and pedestrians only, should be erected across the Thames at Eastwyke Farm, connecting the Abingdon and Iffley Roads. This would not only provide an invaluable inner-city, east-west link but access to the cultural centre and, if possible, to Christ Church Meadow.

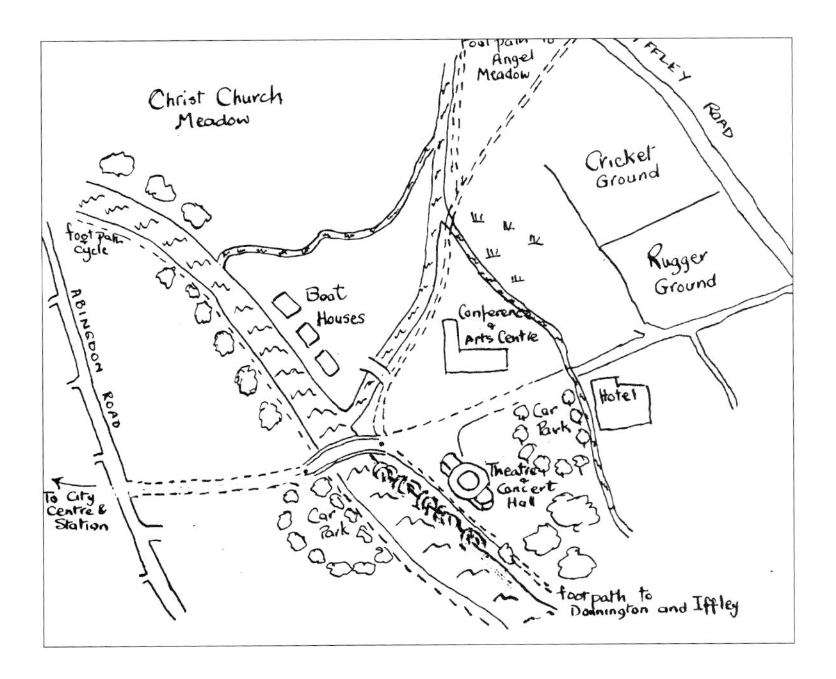

An Uncluttered City

By Maureen Christian

My vision of Oxford is for a city that combines the beauty of a historical city internationally renowned for its fine architecture with the liveliness and buzz of a city which has not atrophied but has grown gracefully to cater for the concentration of young people, tourists and Oxford citizens.

Oxford was the first city in the country to introduce a park and ride scheme and our planning policies have ensured that there has been no increase in car use since the 1970s. However, there are some people who want to turn Broad Street into a car park and St Giles into a bus station and this is not a vision I can share. The pedestrianised Cornmarket has the potential to be one of the most attractive shopping streets in the country but was recently voted the 'Second Worst Street in the Country' on the Today programme. This indicates that we have some way to go although its proximity to the High, which came second in the South East poll for best street, and to the Covered Market, which is a most attractive resource in its own right, shows that the vision could be achieved. The unattractive shopfronts that I campaigned against when I first joined the city council could still be integrated better with the beautiful surroundings we are privileged to enjoy and if the county council can manage to find an attractive, durable and safe way to pave Cornmarket, we would then have a pedestrianised area in the centre of the city that can be enjoyed by residents and tourists and that will encourage further economic benefit.

The city has recently been buried under an excessive number of road signs. In Parks Road there are painted cycles on the road and every few yards there is a pole with a cycle sign on it designating the cycle route as though all cyclists were mentally deficient. Looking north along St Giles, the view of the church and the war memorial is completely obliterated by a huge road sign. The city council employed fingerpost signs that were recommended by the Historic Towns Forum but the recent urban clutter and proliferation of signs has been done by the county council in their role as highway authority. They have even included a dramatic mask on the sign for the Sheldonian Theatre, which is certainly not a theatre in the modern sense. I would like to see a less cluttered environment, which is more sympathetic to our architectural heritage.

The excessive amount of painting on the road surface with different colours and white lines is contrary to aesthetic urban design and combined with the proliferation of bollards, islands, traffic calming and lights is confusing for road users and an eyesore for everyone else. The number of traffic lights at the railway station makes me wonder whether we bought them by the factory-load for a discount. My vision for Oxford does not include highway engineers as urban designers.

The economic pressures on the city from the traders are in danger of destroying the very things that people want to see. The traffic-free day in Broad Street that the Broad Street traders opposed showed how beautiful that street is. We go to Florence and Prague to see beautiful architecture but they would not treat their city centres as unsympathetically as we do ours. We have three of the most beautiful streets in Europe: the High, St Giles and Broad Street. All these need to be seen in an uncluttered state to appreciate the vistas that they can offer. I hope that the county council as the highway authority can take note of the concerns of many of Oxford residents about these three streets. The council must have been made aware of the public feeling roused by the treatment of Cornmarket by the vote in the Today programme.

The city council has tried to ensure improvements by commissioning and paying for a Public Realm Strategy and an urban design brief for the western part of the city by Roger Evans before urban design had become fashionable. I would suggest that the county council read and act on the Public Realm Strategy. Cornmarket could be a most attractive street. It has the Saxon tower of St Michael in the Northgate and the historic building which houses the Laura Ashley shop. It also encompasses the beautiful vista down to Tom Tower and Christ Church.

One of the main concerns in the management of tourism is access to the city centre. It would be possible to improve facilities at the Oxpens coach park for both tourists and coach drivers. With a little imagination, access to the city centre could be vastly improved with a walk by the Castle Mill Stream up through the castle. This would give visitors an introduction to the history of Oxford and ensure the economic success of both the educational centre and the whole castle site. It is imperative that we succeed in having access through the castle site to ensure its incorporation into the tourist trail.

UNTITLED

- like the New High Street shark

Fair Oxford, dear city, our home and our pride
Where a sheikh's ransom buys you a place to reside;
Look up, see the gargoyles we all of us know,
Ignoring the clutter on pavements below.

You risk stumbling over a bollard or tramp
- Look out! Up those steps they have now put a ramp!
Ah, these are the hazards that all of us face
For living in quite such a wonderful place.

There are signs up, to point to the theatres, the station,
Museums, - but not where to find information;
Some signs are not pretty, yet big as a tree,
And obscure the fine buildings our friends came to see.

On foot you'll go shopping with minimal fuss,
Just park on the outskirts and take the green 'bus.
Clutching groceries, clothes, you'll discover you are
Bound to hire a cab to get back to your car

Dick Thomas, 2003

Restoring Oxford's Image

By Jeremy Mogford

I first arrived in Oxford in 1976, not long after my twenty fifth birthday, and opened Browns Restaurant in an old Morris Garage, situated in a seemingly obscure location in the Woodstock Road, yards north of Little Clarendon Street. Many local people said that our chosen site was too far from the city centre to be successful. Luckily they were proved wrong and from the beginning the people of Oxford took Browns to their hearts. Since then I have been involved with quite a number of businesses, all in the same field.

In 1976, I immediately realised that Oxford was a unique, thriving, vibrant, multifaceted city with a healthy mixture of numerous educational institutions, professionals, local industry and a multitude of various businesses. In those days it had a truly amazing selection of independent shops and businesses ranging from shoemakers, jewellers, independent department stores, art galleries, food shops, dairies, printers, haberdashers, antiques shops, restaurants, pubs, bakeries, fashion shops and at its heart, a thriving covered market. I remember them all and I am sure many readers of this book would be able to recall their individual names.

Nearly thirty years later, I look back and consider whether things have changed for the better or worse and what would my ideal vision be for our city in the future. Oxford is perhaps one of the most beautiful cities in Great Britain and could be ranked amongst the best in the world. Yet, is it really thriving and equipped to deal with the future?

Oxford has always attracted large numbers of visitors both from Britain and abroad. People visit the city for many reasons, some with links to the university, others for industry with publishing lately taking an increasingly dominant position and of course there are the foreign tourists who come throughout the year to view this internationally renowned destination. Strangely though Oxford has a reputation as a place where many visitors do not stay for more than a few hours and consequently often do not contribute much income to the local economy. This dilemma has exercised the minds of those involved with the development of Oxford as a tourist destination. Why do people not stay longer and spend more? Is it because there are insufficient hotels or is Oxford too close to London and therefore just a short stop en route for destinations further afield? Is it because deep down the university is not terribly interested in visitors or the local authorities have not addressed their needs and organised a simple and logical method of getting people into what is accepted as a difficult and inaccessible city? This is really a subject in itself and I can only touch on the solution.

Given my experience and background, I know that I should be looking at any future vision from a tourism, leisure, eating and drinking perspective, but one cannot isolate these areas of economic activity. Everything going on in Oxford is inextricably interlinked and to a large extent interdependent. Any thriving business, town or city with a well-balanced local economy requires focused clear direction from its leaders. Whilst I'm sure it could be argued that the university could almost function in isolation, the link between the university and all the other activities gives Oxford its unique character.

Oxford is not what it used to be. It is duller, noticeably less vibrant and its shopping streets are dominated by high street multinationals. Over the last few years it has lost many of its specialist individual retailers.

There has been a general dumbing down and I feel that a sizeable percentage of the more affluent shoppers or visitors has been increasingly discouraged from choosing Oxford as their shopping or leisure destination. Where are the antique shops, art galleries and specialist food shops now? I believe they have gone because their customer numbers have significantly diminished. Why has this happened? The answer is simple, they have been discouraged by council policies. Successive city and county councils have not recognised the special ingredients that are needed to make our city thrive. They have damaged Oxford through misguided transport policies, dogma and a failure to recognise the fact that the unique character of this city needs constant nurturing.

A pavement café in Cornmarket on experimental traffic-free day, 1996.
Photo Genefer Clark

My vision for change is as follows:

1. Big investment should go into park and ride. The sites should become well-designed, totally secure and attractive hubs for all types of transport, incorporating budget hotel accommodation, restaurants, rest rooms, offices and other facilities. All out-of-town coaches and buses would stop at their nearest and relevant park and ride where their passengers would disembark and immediately get on a FREE liveried bus (all painted in the same tasteful colour) which would go to the city centre at frequent intervals. This would dramatically reduce the numbers of half empty buses now dominating and ruining the centre of our city. Car occupants who choose park and ride would do the same. The commercial development of these park and ride areas would pay for many of the changes.

2. The current system of traffic direction and management has to be reviewed as we now have a city effectively cut in two. How does one pick up that elderly aunt from the station and take her to Headington without giving up a frustrating length of time? As an urgent experiment I believe that High Street should be reopened or at least closed for a much shorter time period coinciding with a notional rush hour.

3. All taxis should be the same easily recognised colour, one sympathetic to the city.

4. Cars must be recognised as a legitimate chosen means of transport for some visitors and consequently the standard of car parks must be improved and signage to all car parks indicating position, number of spaces and cost implemented. Car borne visitors are a vital source of income for many of the smaller specialist businesses. If, though, someone chooses to drive into the city during peak times they would pay a high price for the privilege and the city centre rates should be advertised alongside cheaper or free park and ride charges.

5. No parking charges after 6 pm to encourage evening visitors and no charges on Sunday.

6. Parking wardens should be firm and polite and trained as ambassadors for our city. They should collect tariffs with style and pride. Parking money should go to the city and not to private operators.

7. Police should be more visible on our streets and should be more intolerant of antisocial behaviour such as drunkenness and aggressive begging.

8. We need an overlord whose responsibility is the aesthetics of the streets: the state of the pavements, quality of our street furniture, planters, signage, collection of litter and street cleaning.

9. A tourist tax could be considered; perhaps 50p per person for hotel rooms. It is used in many other places to contribute towards a more proactive city tourist office for public relations and the general encouragement of tourism. This could be extended to other tourist attractions. Perhaps colleges should also contribute.

10. Wherever possible, I would like to see a general widening of pavements. The High would be a prime candidate for this. Pavement cafes would help to improve the notion of a cosmopolitan and continental atmosphere.

These are just a few of the policies that I believe would begin to restore the vibrancy and economic activity and would help bring back our lost visitors, making Oxford, once again, pre-eminent amongst British cities. A buoyant local economy combined with the simple laws of supply and demand would automatically provide many of the extra facilities required to meet our needs.

My greatest vision is for Oxford to get the strong local leadership it deserves; a local government that is clear about the priorities required to develop the city economically whilst making the most of its inherent beauty.

Oxford is unique and it deserves more.

A Better Transport System

By Michel Treisman

My vision for transport would require a complete change in Oxford's ambitions for the centre. Present policy is based on a determination to expand shopping whenever and wherever possible, whatever pressure for more transport this may create. Councillors do not acknowledge this as their policy and the issue is seldom discussed in public - expansion is just assumed to be inevitable, or necessary. But my vision is that a conversion occurs; that no more traffic generators are built at the centre; that sites that become available are used for brown field housing, open space and cultural facilities. We would then at least be able to hold the level of traffic where it is, rather than see more pressure for increases and drastic measures to meet them. This restraint is the key and starting-point to maintaining and improving the city as a pleasant place to live in.

To understand the present situation we need to look back at how it has arisen and consider what the future consequences of continuing expansion may be. Policy for the preservation and planning of Oxford is laid down at several levels. Government policy is to preserve the unique historic character of Oxford: their publication *Regional Planning Guidance* for the South East tells us that "historic towns such as Oxford need to be protected from the effects of traffic and excessive urban development and the overall scope for their development is necessarily limited".

Government policy precludes major expansion in Oxford. In conformity with this guidance, the Oxfordshire County Council in its Structure Plans of 1979 and 1998 developed and reaffirmed provisions intended to protect the architectural and historic status of Oxford. The 1979 Structure Plan introduced an imaginative approach to controlling the growth of this city. Departing from the traditional model in which a single large centre is assumed to dominate a wide surrounding area, the county council set out to encourage the development of Oxford's neighbouring country towns so that they could act as counter magnets for new development and so ease the pressure on Oxford. This is defined as the main component of the county's strategy and its consequences are spelled out in several policies, including "employment growth will be particularly restrained in Oxford", and "most industrial, commercial, and other development generating basic employment ... will be steered to Banbury, Bicester, Didcot and Witney".

The 1979 Structure Plan also took account of contemporary needs, stating that "shopping development will be needed in Banbury and Oxford ...to meet the more specialised needs of the populations of [their] wider catchment areas." In an Explanatory Memorandum (May 1987) the county clarified this by stating that "the Council considers that a limited amount of new floorspace can be accommodated within both town centres". The 1998 Structure Plan reaffirms these policies. It states: "The Plan continues the 'country towns' strategy that was first endorsed by the Secretary of State in 1979 with Banbury, Bicester, Didcot and Witney identified as the preferred locations for new development. ... Successive Secretaries of State have stressed that Oxford should not continue to grow indefinitely, that its character and landscape setting should be protected". It notes that whereas the country towns provide "the opportunity to reduce the need to travel through … living and working in the same place", in contrast, "the number of jobs in Oxford is much greater than the size of the resident workforce. This results in large inflows of commuters and puts considerable pressure on Oxford's housing stock.".

These are the policies for Oxford's development that have emerged from the democratic process. But they do not appeal to everyone. There is a body of contrary opinion among many councillors and planners that resents this approach as constraining the proper development of Oxford and that would be much more pleased if the city continued to grow indefinitely. Members of this informal expansionist planning establishment feel that only continued growth can ensure a proper future for Oxford, that it deserves to become a large, an important, city, in whose governance they could be proud to be involved. They rarely oppose our formally adopted policies head-on or broadcast their contrary views. They prefer to pay lip-service to environmentalism, or whatever it is the public may be concerned with at any given time, and under this cover fight targeted battles for particular measures that will contribute to Oxford's proper and desirable growth.

These views arise from assumptions once widely held: that any region will naturally be centred on a great city and that it is the duty and interest of all citizens to expand the size of their city and its domination of the surrounding area. The expansionists do not consider that we are now in a different era in which these views need to be re-thought. That whether and how a city should expand should depend on its particular economic and social circumstances. That what matters is the quality of the environment it provides for its citizens, not a crude substitute index such as the number of people visiting certain shops.

Expansionist views are held by members of all parties and by a tacit agreement they rarely get debated in the political field. This has two advantages. First, the hard graft of working out detailed justifications for these policies, and perhaps failing to produce a convincing account, can be avoided. Second, the risk that the voters, given the opportunity, might actually reject these policies, can be bypassed. Thus, at the last local elections, we were asked to decide between the parties on the basis of the charges they favoured for removing bulky items of rubbish. We were certainly not asked to consider whether a major, and possibly damaging, expansion of the city centre and of Oxford as a whole should be proceeded with. Yet this is the most important issue that faces us now and will face us in coming years.

While the expansionist view is not usually advocated in public, it has long permeated councillors' thinking and determined policy. The Balanced Transport Policy (BTP), published in 1973, illustrates this. This document, the forerunner of the current Oxford Transport Strategy, has often been appealed to as evidence for the primacy the city council gives to the environment. Indeed, at one point the document claimed to reject road-building in principle: building roads just brings more traffic, it says. But what we are asked to forget is that its main practical proposals included the construction of the Westgate multi-storey parking garage and, despite the claimed objection to road building, the creation of a major new radial access road. This was to run from the Western bypass, south of Botley Road, through the green belt, rising at points on embankments thirty feet above the plain, sweeping down into Oxford, to bring a continuous inflow of car-borne shoppers to the new Westgate shopping centre and so ensure its success. That project was pursued for several years but the money required could not be raised. Other proposals were more successful. Over the next few years the council constructed park and ride car parks in or close to the green belt with buses linking them to the centre, another policy claimed to be 'green' but which does not work out that way.

Park and ride was ostensibly, and very plausibly, a scheme to reduce traffic and congestion along our radial roads and in the centre. But in no single case did construction of a park and ride car park in the green belt result in any detectable reduction in traffic down the corresponding roads to the centre. The number of vehicles entering the city centre has oscillated around the same average level since well before the BTP was introduced. The number of vehicles in 1996 was the same as in 1966. If some cars diverted to park and ride, others took their places on the roads to the centre. The effect was that park and ride supported an increase in the number of shoppers visiting the centre at the cost of an increase in the number of journeys to Oxford. The system accommodates about 5000 visits a day, or 1.5 million extra journeys a year, that would not have become habitual in the absence of these car parks.

During the nineties a number of traffic measures were taken culminating, in 1999, in the removal of buses from Cornmarket Street and the exclusion of many cars from High Street, these measures being referred to as the Oxford Transport Strategy (OTS). It is frequently described by councillors as a scheme to reduce traffic at the centre. But at the Inquiry into the OTS, the county's Chief Transport Planner denied that the scheme was intended to reduce traffic: the actual intention was to make the shopping streets more attractive. Those were the terms of reference of the scheme and what it was designed to do. Why then, I asked, did councillors tell us it was a scheme to reduce traffic? Because that was the aspect the public were interested in, he replied.

Following the changes in 1999, business fell and traffic fell. These were not the intended effects, and council officers appealed to other causes, such as the high value of the pound, to explain them. Indeed, in the period preceding these changes, 1997-1999, turnover at the centre was already falling and application of the OTS may merely have hastened this effect. What caused this? Since this decline was not part of a national trend, it is likely to reflect the expansion and increasing attractiveness of centres in neighbouring towns.

If we wish to understand where we are going, it is useful to know where we have come from. What an examination of past actions illustrates is the extent to which a strategy of forcing growth, and increasing traffic for that purpose, has been masked under the guise of a concern for the environment. We can expect this to continue. Why have the planners chosen this course? Councillors offer explanations that are little more than soundbites: "The future of Oxford is retail", they may say. This means almost nothing. Oxford is not an isolated shopping mall but has a complex many-stranded economy; less than 10 percent of jobs are in retail distribution. To give the multiple chains priority over all other economic concerns is not a prescription for a robust future.

Or we are told that "Oxford is growing!". This portentous assertion is intended to lull us into the belief that we face an irresistible force of history and all we can do is accommodate it. This is far from the case. We have a framework of national policy and have been given planning powers, precisely to prevent excessive growth. Another favourite assertion is that "we cannot preserve Oxford in aspic". We are intended to conclude that the only alternative to excessive retail development in the centre is an obscurantist refusal to countenance any change. If so, one does not need to argue for the retail policy; it is obvious.

This is where we are now. What does the future hold? National policy would require us to maintain the present status of Oxford, with adjustments and improvements to the road system where necessary, but no major expansion. But past history suggests this is not what will happen, pressure to "grow" Oxford into a latter day Birmingham will continue. In fact, a further major expansion at the centre is already being pressed ahead. This is a scheme that would more than double the Westgate Shopping Centre in size and would correspondingly entail greater future transport needs.

In 1973, the new Westgate Shopping Centre and Parking Garage opened, two massive, dour and unappealing buildings, out of scale with their surroundings. Westgate was developed by the city council, using public money, and later sold for a fraction of what it is now worth. In 1999 its current owner, Capital Shopping Centres plc, a wealthy developer of out-of-town malls and shopping centres, together with a financial backer, applied for permission to extend Westgate, and in 2000 the city granted this permission. Given the size of the planned extension, the DETR called the Application in and an Inquiry was held in November 2001 (see p9).

The magnitude and impact of the proposals became very clear at this Inquiry. The Applicants' own architectural witness, Robert Adam, called the present shopping centre a "scar across the urban fabric". The extension would have more than doubled that scar: a solid mass of masonry and glass extending some 360m, from Bonn Square at the heart of the retail centre to Thames Street at its edge. It would have been 80m across and at places five or six stories tall, some parts rising above the Local Plan's 60ft limit. The new Westgate would have been by far the largest building in Oxford, its length corresponding to five or six city centre blocks, its footprint two or three times greater than any other construction. Intrusive and immoveable, it would have dominated Oxford's south-west quarter, a physical and psychological barrier between the eastern and western sectors.

The Westgate parking garage would have gone underground, giving way to a monolithic block of shops marching from there to Thames Street, solidly filling an area which in the Local Plan was intended for mixed office and residential development together with "the creation of a public space... to avoid too monolithic an appearance for this very large street block". The northern end of Old Greyfriars Street, which currently separates shopping centre and car park, would have been swallowed up in a glass bubble linking the present shops to its north with the new shops to its south in an unbroken sequence, and functioning as a bus hub to which all city bus routes would be diverted. This triumph of close packing would ensure that passengers emerged into the entrails of Westgate, immediately exposed to its shop windows, to walk its shopping mall before ever they reached our more traditional shops. This planning application was withdrawn in 2003 and a new scheme is being prepared.

If the interests of Oxford's citizens had first priority, the obvious site for the bus hub would be Oxpens, which presently offers an irreplaceable opportunity to allow local buses to terminate alongside the intercity coach services, which should move there from hopelessly under-provisioned Gloucester Green. The site would immediately adjoin the railway station if, as is mooted, it moves there. Oxford would then have the benefits of a universal traffic interchange.

If there is no further major expansion at the centre, then, apart from some rationalisation and improvements, traffic patterns within Oxford should remain much as they are. Outside Oxford we may expect some further increase in congestion as the industries in the science and business parks at the periphery establish themselves. Although new, productive, high-tech industries that will make a contribution to the British economy are very much to be welcomed, given the high congestion on all the approach roads to Oxford, further expansion would be better located at industrial parks in Witney and other nearby towns.

If some form of Westgate Extension goes through, the number of additional shoppers it will require will be a major determinant of traffic in the next decade. The city council had approved 32,000sq m of retail floor space on this site, although the Local Plan allows only 6,500sq m, amounting to an increase in central retail floor space at the centre of 27% at one go. Any such expansion would take an enormous bite out of the custom presently available to other shops at the centre: the Westgate applicants estimated that about 40% of their take would be diverted from elsewhere in the centre. Merely to maintain the present average level of activity would need something like an extra 20,000 shoppers a day, about four times the current capacity of park and ride. This is a rough estimate, but it indicates the scale of the transport problem.

It seems doubtful that all these new shoppers will appear as planned. In their absence the traditional centre of Oxford will suffer. But if against the odds the Applicants prove to be right in their predictions, hordes of new shoppers will come banging on our doors, eager to travel greater distances to get to Oxford. If so, they will run up against the difficulties of getting here. Once again, councillors will demand that we make it easier for shoppers to get to the centre.

The planning establishment has several schemes for meeting this demand. First, better use should be made, they feel, of those "sterile agricultural fields", as they refer to the green belt, which some city councillors are eager to fill with additional and expanded car parks. Some might be decked, doubling their capacity. We can expect more such proposals, in every case supported by the claim that they will reduce traffic into Oxford, though this has never happened yet.

A more innovative proposal is the Guided Transit Express, which one can think of as a substitute for the additional western radial road the city failed to get built in the Seventies. The principle is to use land alongside railway tracks so that buses can run on guide rails along them. The GTE line would run between the Peartree car park in the north and the Redbridge car park in the south. The buses would be able to leave the guided line in the centre and proceed normally through the city. This system would allow many additional buses to carry shoppers from Peartree and Redbridge. At first sight this proposal is a little puzzling, as these two park and ride car parks are already fairly heavily used. It is put forward "to reduce congestion" and it might indeed remove some buses from Abingdon and Woodstock Roads. Even if, in due course, proposals to extend Redbridge and Peartree car parks come forward, the effects would still seem small in relation to the considerable commercial investment the system will require. But the proposal can be better understood when seen in relation to the county's overall transport plans.

The county has a more ambitious scheme yet. It views the further addition of car parks to the green belt with less enthusiasm than some city councillors, as a process which cannot reasonably be taken much further. What it has in mind is more inventive: an extension of the park and ride system in which the car parks need not cluster around Oxford. Thus remote park and ride car parks might be built in Bicester or Witney or other towns where shoppers could leave their cars and from there be bussed to Oxford. These buses might travel directly to the centre, or they could enter the GTE system at Peartree or Redbridge, travelling along the guided rails to the centre. This scheme would extend a new traffic system throughout Oxfordshire, able to carry shoppers from near and far to Oxford. The new travelling public this will create, people who otherwise might simply have shopped in their home towns, will provide a very acceptable additional revenue stream for the bus companies, who have campaigned for bus lanes between the towns and who are working hard to encourage the introduction of the GTE system. And it will be very acceptable to the Department of Transport, who will be happy to be told that more people are using buses and to believe that these schemes therefore provide an innovative method of reducing car use.

It is evident that our future traffic needs will be shaped by the continuing pressure to expand shopping at the centre and that each step will be made under the banner of some worthy environmental purpose.

The policy of expansion as such will certainly never be put before the voters at the local elections. They might ask awkward questions: Who will actually benefit? At what cost to our amenities? And at what extra tax cost to them? Letting all this be debated in public and at elections is something the parties have not sought to do in the past.

What alternatives are there to the expansionist approach? It is difficult for many councillors even to conceive that there might be an alternative, when our system of local government persuades each city and town that it is engaged in an extreme struggle with all the rest for commercial dominance or to protect its own shopkeepers. If reducing transport use throughout the county were indeed given first priority, the key policy to achieve this would be to encourage smaller shopping centres to provide more of the needs of their local customers, so that they would need to travel less often and less far to buy the goods they require.

Such a policy would encourage provision in village shops rather than small towns, and in small towns rather than further distending the cities. But this is not an approach that is likely to be applied by any local politicians unless it is clearly and explicitly adopted as national policy. It is, however, the vision I hold out to those who would like to see a better city, and at the least, no further deterioration in Oxfordshire's traffic.

Transport - Building a Sustainable Future for Oxford's Glorious Past

By Marcus Lapthorn

Reflections

Having lived and worked in many different UK locations, I seem to have been drawn back to Oxford again and again over the years. I have not always actively sought to return here but various opportunities have come along and I have never been able to resist being attracted back to this wonderful city.

My first experience of Oxford was many years ago when a school friend and I cycled around Britain. Oxford was one of our first ports of call and my first and lasting impression was of the wonderful college buildings. It is highly poignant however, that one image of that trip to Oxford was the awful congestion that plagued the city, particularly at the Carfax end of High Street. We are all aware of how that situation became progressively worse in the years that followed.

The reality of living and working in a city where crossing the main shopping street meant literally risking your life in a battle against the traffic, already thankfully seems a fairly distant memory. Nevertheless, I would strongly recommend that any who doubt the wisdom of strategic transport improvements glance through the archives at the photographic reminders of those dangerous and dirty days.

Fortress Oxford

I tend to agree with those who say that Oxford is a city that has two quite different faces and that rarely do the two take time to look at each other. Oxford, like most cities, encompasses areas of extreme deprivation which are generally not far from areas of extreme affluence. Any city that has 39 colleges, two universities, two councils, two bus companies and a whole host of voluntary sector operators is going to be a complex place and, in that respect, Oxford does not disappoint.

The local population of Oxford and, indeed of the county, is acknowledged to be amongst the most intelligent, articulate and vociferous in the country. Necessarily then, achieving change of any kind is difficult and the challenges mounted display a degree of sophistication which would be unrecognisable elsewhere.

Let me take, for example, the 'Streets of Shame' campaign held in autumn 2002. The listeners of Radio 4's Today programme were invited to participate in a competition organised by the Commission for Architecture and the Built Environment to discover the very worst streets in Britain. Oxford's Cornmarket came second behind Streatham High Road in South London.

I find myself wondering whether listeners really believe that Cornmarket is worse than those inner city streets in, say, Brixton, Toxteth or Bradford where drug dealing, prostitution and gun crime are rife, or, as I suspect, are we just witnessing the effects of a higher proportion of Radio 4 devotees than elsewhere displaying their legitimate concerns about the quality of the paving? Either way, this sort of negative publicity is unnecessarily, and largely unfairly, detrimental to the vitality of a beautiful city and is certainly disproportionate to the scale of any perceived problem.

For this reason, achieving any stated objective in the city is not without its pitfalls and at one end of the spectrum are those who wish to see Oxford preserved in time, dedicated only to the pursuit of academic excellence. In this model, shopping and other commercial activity is perceived as something distasteful that only 'other people' do and certainly should preferably do elsewhere. Another grouping is those who wish to erect gates at the end of Abingdon Road, Botley Road and all other arterial routes into the city, allowing access only for cycles and buses.

Meanwhile, Oxford still wrestles with a third significant lobby - the car afficionados who would like to see the city truly opened up for their personal convenience, with other transport modes, public transport, cyclists and pedestrians, relegated to 'somewhere else'.

Unpaid Advisers

With this veritable army of unpaid 'advisers' on hand to challenge every move made by the local authorities and the private sector, it is no wonder that major improvement objectives take rather longer to reach fruition here than in most other places. I would of course be the first to acknowledge that delay is sometimes a jolly good thing. Most of us would, for example, thank the academic community of Oxford for managing to frustrate the idea of building a relief road across Christ Church Meadow.

Clearly then, one person's progress is another's disaster. This is best exemplified by recent events surrounding the proposed redevelopment of the Westgate Shopping Centre. The vast majority of people in Oxford relished the prospect of improved shopping facilities and a general upgrade in the quality of the fabric of that quarter of the city, including the long-awaited removal of buses from Queen Street. Yet these aspirations were dashed when the Office of the Deputy Prime Minister rejected the proposals, following lobbying on behalf of a number of minority interests. How long can this kind of general 'no-go' approach continue before investors give up on Oxford entirely? The view of one potential investor, commenting on the situation here, was telling: "It is just too difficult... and at a time when other cities are crying out for infrastructure investment."

So what is the picture that I have so far painted of this unique city? A city of extremes, perhaps, with the majority of people not participating in the democratic process and just hoping that an elusive 'someone' will get on with things and make the city a pleasanter and more user-friendly place?

A Centre of Excellence

The implementation of the Oxford Transport Strategy (OTS) won Oxfordshire County Council immense accolades from central government including recognition of Oxford as a Centre of Excellence in transport thinking. Interestingly, this issue, more than any other, will split opinion amongst readers. Many will feel that such an award was well deserved but, possibly, that the OTS did not go far enough in improving the transport infrastructure of the city. Others will express utter amazement and frustration that the Government should applaud a system to which they are violently opposed.

Although there are few certainties in life, one thing is guaranteed. The population of Oxfordshire is set to grow substantially, particularly with the further development of certain county towns, such as Bicester, Didcot, Abingdon and Witney. Oxford will remain the economic hub of the county and the desire of individuals to avail themselves of the commercial, leisure and retail facilities which the city can offer should be accommodated. It is far preferable and, it seems to me, self-evident that we need to plan sensibly for growth so that it can be managed without detriment to the city.

Oxford is a historic city and simply does not have the capacity to absorb more car traffic. Nor is growth in the use of private vehicles in the city desirable given the environmental damage already caused to its architectural fabric and the general health of its population by emissions. Equally, it is deeply unrealistic of those lucky enough to live within the city's boundaries to expect all visitors and commuters to walk or cycle. The only feasible answer is improved public transport and this needs to be more widely recognised.

No Going Back

I have come across individuals who are keen to support public transport infrastructure improvements and the encouragement of 'other people' to use it, thus leaving the roads clear for their car journey. The public, in general, tend to be schizophrenic about improvements in traffic management; they lobby for wider, faster roads yet complain bitterly if such roads are to be developed anywhere near their own houses. We are all aware that car use is on the increase throughout the country but Oxford is taking the lead in standing firm against a very vocal car lobby and continuing to build a city linked by efficient bus routes.

The statistics show quite clearly that bus use in the city continues on an upward trend. Anecdotal evidence also indicates that visitors and commuters vastly favour public transport, where it works, over traffic gridlock.

Oxford has always been at the forefront of transport thinking and has long pre-empted the national public transport agenda. It was, for example, the first city in Britain to embrace the park and ride concept - a service now so popular that a fifth park and ride site at Water Eaton has been recently opened, with another, Thornhill, being extended.

Continuous improvement is vital to sustain this leadership position and to ensure that the city can meet the demands of future journeys. Despite all efforts, nationally, road traffic is set to increase by 22% by 2010 from 2000 levels and vehicle-generated pollution is set to soar. Other major cities - Bristol, Edinburgh, Birmingham and Manchester - look likely to follow London's example of introducing congestion charging in order to tackle a traffic problem that is simply economically crippling. In stark contrast, Oxford is one of the few places where the future looks brighter because of sensible and early planning; our task now is to ensure sustainability.

To achieve this, passengers need to have their journeys made as simple as possible. The city also needs to ensure that the public have the services that they want and need, serving appropriate destinations and at a reasonable, affordable cost. Extensive research shows that there are five key factors which influence passengers' choice:

- Regularity of services
- Reliability of services
- Quality of vehicles
- Location of stops and quality of shelters
- Provision of accurate travel information

The future

In order to accommodate these choice factors and to anticipate the growth in demand for services, many in the city have taken a long, hard look at the future options. A key element is the need to eliminate the problems of congestion that can still adversely affect Oxford's otherwise world-class bus network.

Photo courtesy First Group, Leeds

It is against this backdrop that the plan to bring guided buses to Oxford was conceived, drawing on best practice experience from such places as Adelaide in Australia and Essen in Germany. Closer to home, the concept has proved extremely successful in Leeds and Bradford, where the West Yorkshire Passenger Transport Executive continue to work on further extensions to the programme.

Feedback from Leeds indicates that within two years of their A61 scheme opening, it was enjoying a 50% increase in patronage and around half of those passengers had a car available to them. Over half of those surveyed said that the service had greatly improved, 30% were using the bus more than previously and 30% were wholly new passengers to the bus network - a stunning achievement.

So, given all of the social and political factors which I have described as prevalent in Oxford, is a guided bus network an appropriate scheme for the city? Those involved with the project come from a diverse range of backgrounds and their tremendous combined experience and expertise suggest that it is. Similarly, passengers who participated in an informal survey about the proposals unanimously expressed their support. The Guided Transit Express (GTE) concept was first suggested by the Oxford Bus Company. The Board of Directors now consists of representatives of the city and the county councils, Oxford University and Oxford Brookes University, the city's transport operators and Oxford's retail and business communities. GTE for Oxfordshire Ltd was formed in late 1998.

Expressway Oxford

Expressway Oxford is the new operating name for the Guided Transit Express scheme, the guided bus initiative that is planned to provide the next phase of a balanced transport strategy for the city. Essentially, Expressway will offer specially constructed, segregated bus guideways largely on disused railway land, running alongside the main line. The guided bus system will have high quality, easy access and low emission vehicles connecting with the conventional road network to travel to other destinations off guideway.

Expressway is expected to bring tremendous benefits by:

- Enabling fast and reliable journeys into central Oxford from the edge of the city and beyond. A segregated, congestion-free track will allow faster journeys into Oxford, where there will be an Expressway stop at the railway station. Vehicles will then run on-street, with priority over general traffic, to the heart of the city.

- Transforming the speed and the quality of the park and ride network by serving the Redbridge and Peartree sites - services will be faster, more frequent and with greater capacity.

- Extending, off guideway, beyond the city to Water Eaton park and ride and surrounding towns including Abingdon, Bicester and Didcot, forming the backbone of a co-ordinated transport system for the whole county. The guided bus system will link with existing bus and rail infrastructure to offer high quality direct or connecting services to surrounding towns.
- Facilitating future guideway extensions to, say, Witney, Heyford Hill and Headington.
- Creating a better local environment by the use of the operators' most environmentally-friendly buses.

Photos courtesy First Group, Leeds

It is clear that in order to achieve the maximum benefit from the Expressway proposals, they need to be properly co-ordinated with the other important ongoing and potential developments along the possible route. I am pleased to say that there is significant, high-level interest in ensuring a workable approach to a sustainable future for the city. Indeed, transport options to Oxford railway station, the Westgate Shopping Centre, the castle/prison site redevelopment, the Oxpens quarter generally and Oxford Science Park would all be beneficially improved by the Expressway plans. It is clear that this serves a dual purpose of enhancing the attractiveness of those developments as destinations whilst, at the same time, increasing the use of the guided bus network.

Consultation

The consultation process is a vital element of the work on the Expressway project and I have already outlined the unique character of Oxford in terms of opposition to change. Experience teaches that the best consultative programmes work with the local community to deliver mutual benefits. The British Airports Authority avoided a Public Inquiry into their expansion plans at Gatwick Airport precisely because they worked closely with residents to achieve a mutually acceptable outcome. By listening to the underlying concerns of the community they were able to find a workable, negotiated way forward that did not thwart BAA's overriding aspirations for the site. I am very keen that this approach is adopted generally in Oxford but it requires a constructive and truly consultative, rather than purely negative, attitude from consultees.

Conclusion

All in all, this is a highly complex project and obtaining legal powers can be a lengthy process but, if approved, the current intention is to open the Expressway in Oxford in 2009. Oxford deserves on-going commitment to its sustainability and vitality by sensible accommodation of predicted growth and better public transport must be at the heart of this commitment. I am hopeful that this project will allow the city to maintain its reputation as a centre of excellence in transport thinking and that those who subscribe to the Fortress Oxford or giant car park visions of its future will recognise the social and economic realities facing us.

Expressway Oxford is one element of a matrix of investment programmes scheduled for the coming years, all designed to enhance the quality of life for those who live, work and socialise in the city. They will shape the future fabric of the place and enable it to retain its historic appeal. My plea is that all sections of the community engage with the possibilities of the future, by way of constructive involvement, as a means of retaining the best of the past.

The views expressed are personal to the author and should not be taken to represent the position of any organisation with which I am, or have been, involved.

A Green and Pleasant City

By John Thompson

Relative to other cities of comparable size, Oxford has an extremely high proportion of open space, the majority being concentrated alongside the Thames and Cherwell rivers. These riverside corridors bring the countryside right into the heart of the city, providing delightful walks with a strong rural character. This special identity is constantly under threat from adjacent development and changing farming practices. It is vital that trees on the fringe of the meadows are maintained and reinforced where necessary so that surrounding buildings are screened. Willow pollarding and appropriate hedgerow management are also key elements in ensuring the distinctiveness of these water meadows. Grazing and hay cutting are the best ways of maintaining the flowery sward, especially the fritillaries, the most exotic of all the water meadow flowers.

Mill Stream Walk
Photo John Thompson

While the city has an abundance of open spaces, they are not always satisfactorily linked with footbridges and paths. A bridge across the Cherwell from the Iffley Fields into Christ Church Meadow would enable walkers and cyclists from the east to reach the city centre avoiding noisy and congested roads. Other rural corridor routes that could be improved are the Cherwell valley where better footpaths are required, Hinksey Meadows and from Hinksey Park through Grandpont to the ice rink. The cycle/footbridge across the northern bypass has opened up a vital link between the Sunnymead open spaces and Cutteslowe Park.

Weeping Willow, Fisher Row, Oxford
Photo John Thompson

To safeguard the special character of the meadows, indigenous planting should be undertaken adjacent to new developments, especially in the case of out-of-town shopping facilities and park and ride sites. The new one at Water Eaton, with its native tree and shrub planting, sits very well in the landscape. Open space in rural areas requires a different management regime from the conventional horticultural practices undertaken in the city's more formal parks and gardens. Regular grass cutting and the use of exotic non-native planting should be avoided. Wolvercote Green, previously regularly cut, is being transformed into a rich wildlife habitat as a result of new management practices drawn up in consultation with English

Nature. The grass is cut once a year for hay, resulting in a greater variety of wild flowers which will benefit insects and birds. Ultimately, it is intended to erect post-and-rail fencing and introduce cattle grazing.

For biodiversity and wildlife, grazing is the most appropriate method of managing the meadows that comprise the city's landscape setting. There are, however, many practical problems, such as gates being left open, fences damaged, worrying of livestock by dogs and dumping of rubbish. To encourage grazing, meetings of various government countryside agencies are being arranged with local landowners, including Oxford Preservation Trust and Oxford City Council, to discuss levels of grant support and management practices. In the Chilswell valley, an area of rough grassland is grazed by dexter cattle, which encourages wildlife and prevents invasion by scrub. At Stockwell, Oxford Preservation Trust's garden on Boars Hill, sheep are used to graze the grassland providing the right circumstances for orchids to flourish. There is considerable demand for horse grazing pastures around the city and because horses are selective grazers concentrating on the finer grasses, great care is necessary to ensure that coarse grasses and rank weeds such as thistles and nettles do not take over. There is the potential to use rare breeds for grazing, like the old English long horn cattle that are such a delightful spectacle in Christ Church Meadow.

The jewel in the crown of the city's open spaces is Port Meadow with its dramatic changes throughout the year. Golden buttercups in summer and silver water in the winter, with the added attraction of the livestock and birds, make it a uniquely vibrant space. Recent development along the canal on the eastern boundary has intruded into the view and the pollarded willows are not sufficiently tall to screen the houses; larger trees need to be added to achieve adequate screening. The Binsey poplars are a vital element and it is essential that the trees that have been blown down in recent storms are replaced. The Civic Society has been involved with the replanting programme and ensured that the rare native black poplars are used, as many of the existing trees are hybrid poplars. The planting of more hawthorn to reinforce those adjacent to the marina is desirable as it would reduce the visual clutter of the boats and buildings.

The wild habitats are an essential part of the city's natural landscape. In an intensely farmed county like Oxfordshire they are particularly welcome.

What would the world be, once bereft
Of wet and of wildness? Let them be left,
O let them be left, wildness and wet,
Long live the weeds and the wilderness yet.

Gerard Manley Hopkins.

The Sites of Special Scientific Interest (SSSIs), with which Oxford is well endowed, provide the wild experience. The Lye Valley with its steep sided slopes, reeds and ponds is an exciting wilderness which could be improved by better footpaths and interpretative information; the same applies to Rock Edge in Headington, the site of an old quarry. It is important that natural habitat is not compromised by development and that management plans of the various sites are drawn up to ensure that biodiversity is encouraged. The Character Assessment Report of Oxford in its Landscape Setting recently produced for the city council will be useful in ensuring that development is sympathetic to the landscape. The 'Town Green' on the Trap Grounds with its wetland and woodland is an important addition to the city's wildlife habitats. The park and ride car parks could be much improved by nature conservation management with interpretative boards explaining the flora and fauna. Currently they are inadequately maintained and make a poor impression on visitors.

To promote understanding of wildlife and nature conservation, the city's Countryside Service organises a programme of annual events in the 28 nature parks it manages around Oxford such as Project Sparrowhawk which takes place in the summer for schoolchildren and the Working Woodland in Brasenose Wood publicising woodland management. A number of publications are available from the Countryside Service including: *A Guide to Shotover Country Park; Oxford's Countryside*; *A Guide to Oxford's Nature Parks* and *Helping Oxford's Wildlife.*

Many of the parks and open spaces lack facilities for young and old and are managed in an unsustainable way. More and better play facilities should be a priority as a meeting place for children and parents. Greater diversity of habitat creates a much more interesting experience for visitors and the short grass and lollipop tree feature of many parks should be avoided. A reduction in grass cutting frequency would encourage more diversity of plants supporting insects and birds; the edges of playing fields could become countryside and a natural experience for dog walkers and other users; costs would be reduced. In some areas, woodland can be established as at Foxwell Drive, where the trees reduce noise from the bypass and create a valuable wildlife corridor, linking Court Farm with Dunstan Road. There, tree planting, bulb planting and improvements to the stream and the creation of ponds have transformed what was previously a sterile place into a wildlife haven, with exciting seasonal variation.

Trees are the predominant natural feature in the city's landscape setting. However, it is important that they are prevented from taking over open space so that the balance of solids to voids is maintained. Thinning of planting is vital to ensure people can see around and not feel threatened. For example the planting at Grandpont Park needs thinning as it is becoming intimidating, especially at night. There is always concern when trees are felled so it is essential that plans for management and replacement are prepared. At Shotover Country Park, a replacement plan is in place that allows for the felling of birch so that the underlying heather is able to regenerate; heathland is rare in Oxfordshire so it is therefore important to the biodiversity of the park. At Binsey, there was much debate over the replacement of the chestnut avenue which was diseased. The trees were all felled in one go but half the trees could have been felled and replaced, with the remaining trees being felled and replaced in ten years. Ideally an uneven age structure of trees should be achieved so that they are not all mature at the same time.

In addition to the native vegetation in the rural areas, the city's gardens are rich in exotic imported trees. The North Oxford garden suburb is especially impressive and the trees and shrubs soften the architecture and add contrasting colour and texture. A leaflet entitled *The Gardens of the North Oxford Victorian Suburb* is available from the city planning department listing the plants, so that owners are aware of the appropriate species to use when undertaking replanting. The unique character of this early garden suburb is thus maintained. New planting in Headington Park and Bury Knowle Park is being done to ensure the continuity of the tree cover. At Hinksey Park, an avenue of over-mature and dangerous balsam poplars has been replaced with whitebeams. In many areas of the city the pavements are too narrow for planting, so the front

Bury Knowle Park, Oxford
Photo John Thompson

Sweet Gums in Gloucester Green
Photo John Thompson

garden is the ideal location to plant, introducing colour and seasonal change to a street. The Forest of Oxford Group has produced a leaflet entitled *Your Front Garden*, listing suitable trees and shrubs.

The Centre of Culture status in 2008 is an excellent opportunity for more creative community activities, for facilities to be provided in open spaces and for a more co-ordinated approach. Burgess Field Nature Park, adjacent to Port Meadow, is an area of young woodland and rough meadow, ideal habitat for deer and birds especially birds of prey, and nesting boxes could be added to encourage owls. The mown grass rides would make excellent sculpture trails and some of the sculpture could be made of thinnings from the woodlands. Students from Brookes and the Ruskin School of Art could participate. Headington Park is also suitable for sculpture and a new entrance could be established to link it with Headington Hall; the old dairy would make an excellent community arts workshop. Parks such as South Park and Cutteslowe are ideal for music, theatre and major events. The possibility of establishing community centres, libraries and art galleries in parks should also be investigated.

There is a need for greater community involvement with parks and open space. The local community should be involved with producing management plans. Manzil Way Gardens by the Cowley Road has been entirely remodelled for greater public use. The local community and police in partnership with the Oxford City Parks Department have undertaken measures to deter drug and alcohol users and transformed the park into an attractive place for shoppers and local residents, as well as being a venue for street markets, events and the annual East Oxford Carnival. The Oxford Urban Wildlife Group has developed and manages the Boundary Brook Nature Park in East Oxford which has a range of habitats including woodland, a pool and flowery meadow; the Elder Stubbs Group has developed similar habitats on allotment land next to the Cowley Road. There is enormous potential for the development of more open space run by voluntary groups with funding from the Trust for the Oxford Environment and Section 106 money obtained by the planning department as a contribution from developers.

The Forest of Oxford Group enables schools, businesses and community groups to undertake tree planting in parks, open spaces and around buildings. Recent projects were a community orchard next to the Trout car park with the Wolvercote Tree Group, trees in Cowley Road with the Cowley Tree Group and tree planting at the Headington Quarry Community Centre. Publications comprise a leaflet on front garden planting and a tree trail leaflet for the city centre. Proposed projects involve trees for Cornmarket Street and Broad Street, nature parks for park and ride car parks and improvements to Green Road roundabout.

While the city has an abundance of water, visitors have limited access to it. The Oxpens Park by the ice rink, bounded to the south by the Thames and to the east by the Castle Mill stream, has enormous potential and the proposed new railway station at Oxpens and the ample nearby parking would make it easily accessible. A public building of excellent architectural quality, with facilities for the arts and sciences, together with a café and restaurant could transform the Oxpens Park into a delightful waterside amenity within walking distance of the city centre. This could be linked by a footpath alongside the Castle Mill stream to the open space at the castle development. The car park opposite Nuffield College is an ideal site for canal boat moorings with shops and restaurants and flats above, overlooking the water. Canal visitors would be provided with an exciting approach to the historic city.

The city centre is short of high quality public spaces and Broad Street, surrounded by some of the city's finest architecture, could provide the city with a splendid meeting place. The street has enormous potential as a major European urban space. Bonn Square is neglected and underused; paving, floral displays, lighting and better access, with the addition of a refreshment kiosk, could transform it into a delightful garden to sit in and watch the world go by. Gloucester Green would be much improved by a central water feature, which would introduce light and sparkle and create an appropriate focal point.

The city's spaces could play a much more important part in its life and help to make it a more inclusive place for residents, visitors, shoppers and members of the universities. It is important that people are able to contribute towards the enhancement and improvement of the city's spaces and to achieve the maximum benefit from them. The rich legacy of wonderful architecture, rivers, water meadows, parks and gardens needs to be better appreciated and enjoyed.

Whitebeam trees at Magdalen College
Photo John Thompson

The View from a Wildlife Garden

By Priscilla Waugh

Without visionaries, our society is a dull one. We have to have visionaries – to aim for the stars. Inevitably, in a democratic society, we would end up with less, even with mediocrity, because people will aim or vote for what they believe to be achievable, rather than for what they truly want. But to aim for mediocrity is a sad option for anyone who cares about the future. In Oxford, with its incomparable human history, it is unthinkable.

So it is here, in this most quintessentially English of cities that I hope we might foment a gentle revolution. We might think more and do less. Think more and buy less. My vision of 21st century Oxford is of a city based on the highest thought and the simplest of lifestyles. Here, in an Oxford whose city fathers are making a brave attempt to help us rethink the supposed freedom the private motor car has inflicted on us, we might reach further into the future and rethink the other supposed blessings we have been granted by modern science. Before we drive off to the out-of-town hypermarket or garden centre, we might just take another look at our private Arcadia and wonder why the butterflies are no longer in evidence, why the once-ubiquitous house sparrows no longer descend in flocks to squabble over the scraps on the lawn or why the song thrush has been largely silenced. We might scratch from our shopping list the peat, the all-in-one growth accelerator, the lawn fertilizer, the insecticides and the plastic sacks. We might, in this city famed for joined-up thinking, just pause to consider ourselves as part of the whole.

If you were to take a journey across the UK in a hot air balloon you would see that the British Isles, described by the Romans as bejewelled by sparkling rivers, has further the benefit of a broadly north-south axis. Thus results its naturally diverse vegetation: from wild heather-clad moors, rugged mountains and wetlands in the north, through lakes and peaks to rolling hills, fine pastureland and deciduous forests towards the south. The particularly kindly landscape of southern England has been further tamed by centuries of husbandry into a charming landscape divided by hedgerows and canals into a patchwork of fields and copses.

Note the word 'divided'. The dividing lines, be they hedgerows, fences, waterways or railway embankments, have for long been used as highways by native flora and fauna, making their way from one feeding or breeding ground to the next. These ad hoc highways are beloved of conservationists, who call them 'green corridors.' As one can well imagine, the grubbing up of ancient hedgerows, the demolition of dry stone walls and the loss of field margins to make way for the present vast prairies of rape seed and grain have played havoc with the ability of wild communities to move on in times of food shortages or habitat destruction, or simply to migrate in order to replenish a diminishing gene pool.

Crossing any major conurbation, you might be surprised to find that by far the most impressive of these green corridors comprises domestic gardens. Something like 80% of British homes have their own gardens. The total area of these gardens outnumbers by almost two to one the acreage given over to the national and local Nature Reserves combined and this vast criss-crossing green superhighway is largely a result of the great British gardening tradition.

Before we become too complacent, however, regarding our own private well-managed piece of urban parkland, let's pause and be grateful to those who are too preoccupied with the rest of their lives to bother about doing the garden. The resultant untidy patches of bramble, nettle, thistles and buddleia support a wide diversity of urban wildlife and are at least as useful – if not more – than our striped green swards and designer bird tables. Their primary value is that they provide food sources uncontaminated by the army of chemicals we spend our weekends browsing through on the shelves at Homebase.

But, on the whole, we are a nation of gardeners and here in Oxford each of the colleges of England's most ancient university has a garden planned and tended by the world's finest.

Now, I'm not for a moment going to imagine that those in charge of this extraordinary heritage are going overnight to forswear the habits of a lifetime spent in professional horticulture. I am more than willing to admit that their knowledge of plant needs and habitats is vastly superior to mine but whereas their primary function is to enhance the gravitas of their illustrious buildings, we could perhaps take a broader view of our responsibilities to the more humble of our fellow creatures.

Everything we do has an impact. It may be that Gaia, in her infinite grace, will correct our errors, but as thinking beings it is surely incumbent on us to limit our interference with a perfect system. Once we accept that slug pellets, blue as they may be to discourage birds, will enter the food chain anyway, albeit second-hand via the ingestion of semi-comatose molluscs, we might decide that we can afford to share a certain amount of our produce with them. However, if they overstep the boundaries of common decency, we might surround vulnerable plants with a substance they will not cross, like gravel or eggshells, or invest in a living predator courtesy of a supplier of biological garden controls or install slug pubs to persuade ourselves that our biggest bugbear will die happy. But of course, slugs are part of our perfect world. We are apt to forget about the interdependence of species; that those we love, perhaps in this case toads or hedgehogs, often depend for their survival on those we don't.

And we might rethink our infatuation with glamour. Do we really want these sterile blooms of exotic or even genetically modified species at the expense of the elusive scents and insects of the traditional English cottage garden? Do we really prefer these immaculate but silent lawns to the song of thrush and blackbird? Do we miss the butterflies that used to decorate our borders enough to stop poisoning their food?

Why have we forgotten the pleasure of compost? Inexplicably, we spend vast amounts of money buying and transporting artificial fertilizers and magic grow-more, grow-fast, grow-huge potions for our personal paradise when it will naturally provide all it needs for its replenishment. Composting is recycling at its most perfect. It is about the continual interchange of molecules between different states of matter. Ashes to ashes, dust to dust; the concept of recycling is truly as old as the hills. We should be passionate about compost. In the Oxford of my vision, inner city citizens will be delighted to have their biodegradable waste collected (in paper sacks, not plastic) and they may even be pleased to pay for the service, knowing that, in return, they will have access to the finest possible growing medium produced on their behalf at a municipal centre by an enlightened city council. At present, the United Kingdom lags far behind most of Europe when it comes to dealing with the valuable resource of its waste. Why?

From your balloon, looking down on my garden in the middle of a West Oxford council estate, you will see that it is just beginning this part of its incarnation. I say 'this part of its incarnation' because of course it is not really 'my' garden at all. It was someone else's garden before I came and before that it was part of a farm orchard. Before that it had another life and before that another. I am just the person entrusted with its present care.

But I do have plans for it. They include everything necessary for a wild garden: pond, hedgerow, meadow and woodland. They could, in fact, be the attributes of its original state. You might wonder at my enthusiasm, given that my self-sown woodland trees of hazel and oak are a bare half-metre high. My hedgerow of hawthorn, blackthorn, briar, holly, spindle, guelder and dogwood, a year into its life, is even less impressive and my meadow, pond and orchard are all still in the infant stage, but that's fine by me. I couldn't envisage a greater pleasure than watching them evolve. I adore my wilderness. Failure is irrelevant. It's all a learning process and if plants don't survive, then I shall assume they're not the right plants and try again with something else. Whatever is meant to grow here will surely grow.

Just one more thing before we alight from this balloon. Let's cast our eyes again over the whole picture. We are not owners of this land. The responsibility of caring for our patch is not onerous: we can do as much or as little as we wish but we must be careful not to abuse the privilege of our stewardship.

Part III

•••••

Forecasts

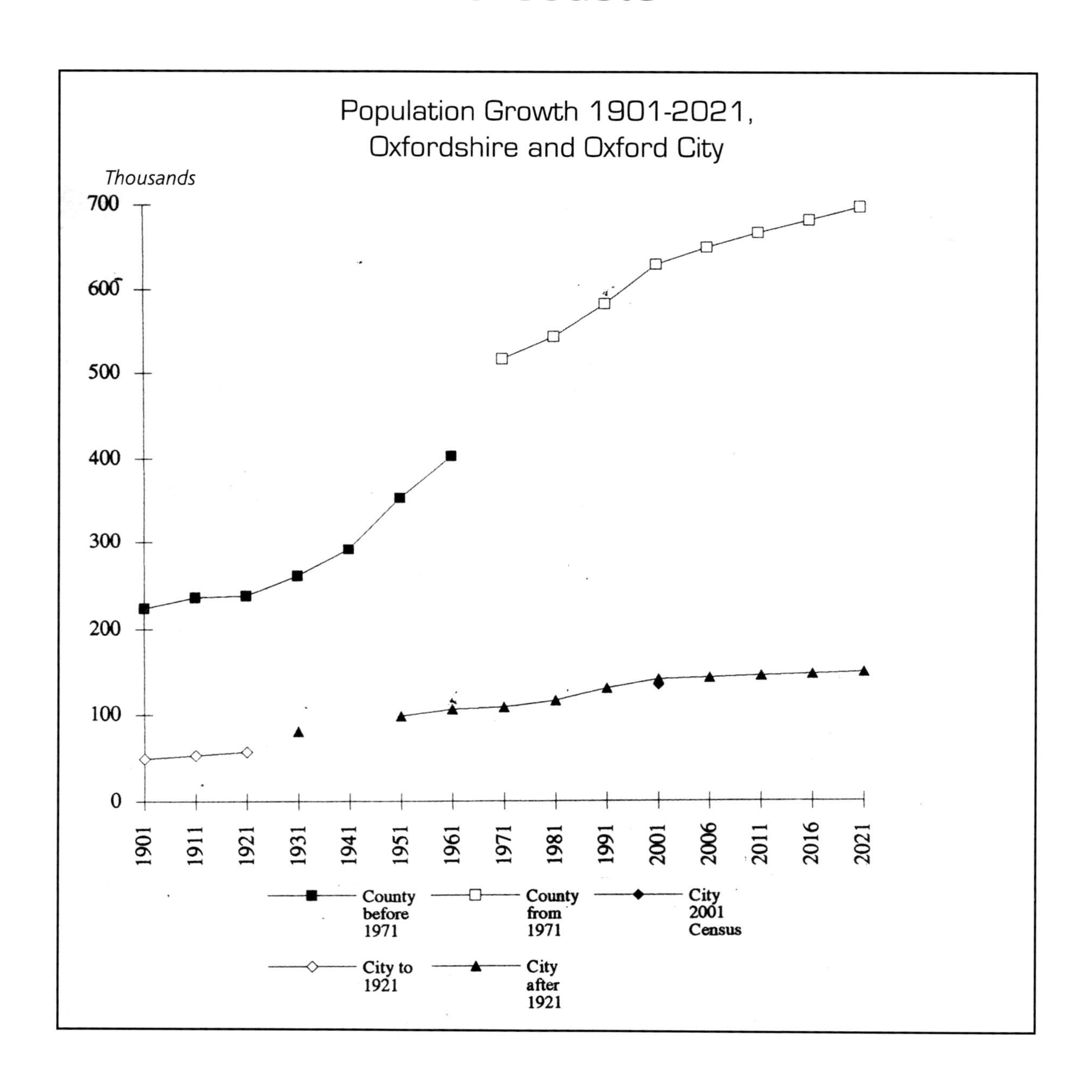

Oxford's Changing Population - A Glimpse of the Future

By David Coleman

Ideally, in a vision of Oxford's future population we should say what we should like to happen. In reality, any visions we have need to be closely related to what is most likely to happen, based on the best projection we can make of present trends. Our ability to manipulate the population's size, structure and distribution is severely limited. However, a forecast of the population's future may help guide policy decisions.

Problems in forecasting the future

How can we tell what will happen next? Demographers do not have the best of reputations for forecasting the future, in which they are in the good company of economists and political scientists. But some of the elements of future change are already apparent in today's society. Some are built into the age-structure of today's population. Many of these are common to the whole country. While Oxford has some interesting special features, like its large student numbers, its population characteristics are not startlingly different from most other places. The local scene is a variant of the national one.

Oxford and its County at the beginning of the 21st Century

We are in an odd position of uncertainty about the population of the city of Oxford in 2001 and subsequently, as indeed we are about the population of the whole of the United Kingdom. The 2001 census revealed that the UK population was about one million people short of the population estimates for the same year. A number of urban areas have consequently been assigned population totals considerably smaller than those they had previously accepted.

Thus Oxford is declared to have had a population of 134,248 instead of the previous figure for 2001 of 141,000. This shortfall is not accepted by the local authority, nor indeed by others, including this author. Among other things, it will reduce the Revenue Support Grant for Oxford. The arguments are complex but essentially the Office for National Statistics (ONS) claims that the 2001 census must be infallible because of the huge technical and financial resources devoted to it. The ONS insists that the error must lie instead in an over-estimate of the 1991 census and a gross undercount of UK citizens leaving the country (for which there is no direct evidence). Accordingly, population estimates back to 1981 are being revised downwards, although the original ones are shown opposite in the absence of new figures for Oxford. This revision affects predominantly white males aged between 15-50, one of many reasons for finding these new figures deeply implausible as no one seems to know where on earth these missing 760,000 white males are hiding.

Whatever the real total, about 30,000 are a mobile population of students, many resident for less than half the year. Of these in 2002, 17,400 belonged to the ancient university, the rest to Oxford Brookes and to the many other educational establishments. Probably no comparable town has such a fluid population, which makes a marked input on the age-structure during term time. The city comprises just a fifth of the population of the county (628,000) to which it belongs (see p.130).

At the beginning of the 19th century, the municipal borough was just one tenth of the city's present size, scarcely 12,000 strong, in a (then smaller) county of 112,000 inhabitants. At the beginning of the 20th century, the now parliamentary borough had grown to 49,000 and its county to 181,000. Can we expect a further radical expansion to transform our city and county during the century which is to come?

Almost certainly not. Changes there will be, but they will be less dramatic and more subtle, some with features familiar to the 20th century, others quite new. The radical changes in population, society and economy since those days, which Oxford and its county shared with the rest of Europe, are over. In respect of population, the transformation, known as the 'demographic transition' saw a family size of five or six children in the 19th century fall to less than two in the late 20th century and expectation of life at birth of scarcely 40 years nearly double to 78 (76 for men, 80 for women) today. The death rate began its, initially very faltering, decline from the middle of the 18th century while the birth rate did not begin to fall at the national level until the 1870s. That ushered in an era of unprecedented population growth which multiplied the national population tenfold from 5 million in 1700 to the 50 million in 2000.

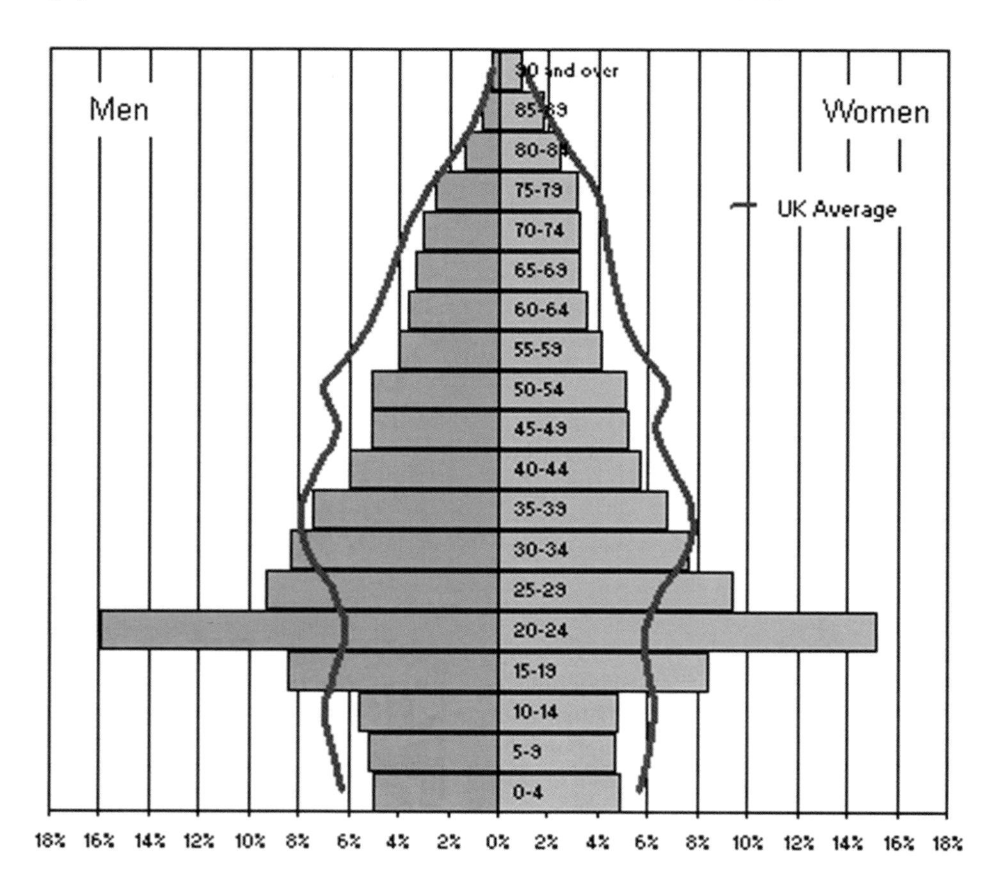

Oxford City's Age Structure in 2002

The demographic transition is over, birth and death rates are nearly in balance again as they were in previous times. The tenfold expansion of Oxford's numbers since 1801 and its threefold growth since 1901 will never be repeated. Instead, more modest growth will come from other sources, mostly migration, and the population will change its character in new ways.

Surviving in Oxford

Oxfordshire's higher than average social profile, its position in the warmer south and its excellent medical facilities give it lower death rates than the national average and have done so since such analysis began in 1851. Standardised for age structure, the death rate for Oxfordshire in 1998 was 91% of the national average and that for the city, 85%.

Ageing – a certain future

Fewer babies and longer lives bring population ageing. This is an inevitable part of the future. The present age structure, inherited from the numbers of births and deaths over the last 100 years, cannot be maintained even if birth and death rates remained the same as they are today, which they are unlikely to do. Even a return to replacement fertility would not preserve the existing age structure, although it would create a stable population distribution more favourable to the management of population ageing. In this respect, Oxfordshire is little different from the rest of Britain, although the city's lower birth rate would by itself generate an older population more quickly were it not for the rejuvenating effect of a large student population. The 1996-based local and regional population projections only extended to the year 2021. However, these showed the proportion of Oxfordshire's population aged 65 and over increasing from 87,300 in 2001 to 126,000 in 2021 – from 13.9% to 18.2%. In the city, the corresponding numbers were projected to be from 12.7% to 14.4%. New local population projections, revised downwards in order to fit the 2001 census, will not be available for some time. This is hardly a demographic time bomb and indeed such devices are much more prone to go off in the media than in real life. However, the acceleration of population ageing projected for Britain in general increases substantially after 2026 thanks to the retirement of the baby boom cohorts born in the 1950s to the 1970s. These will take the national percentage of the over 65s to at least 25% and the figure in Oxford can scarcely be much less. Nonetheless, that is a relatively benign outcome compared with most European countries.

Ethnic minority populations in Oxford and Oxfordshire

Other local processes may increasingly differentiate Oxford from its more rural surroundings. Most notable of these is the rise of immigrant and ethnic minority populations, from the Asian, African and West Indian Commonwealth countries and other parts of the non-European world. These populations, statistically negligible in the early 1950s nationally, as in Oxford, have now increased to 7% nationally by 2000. Ethnic minority populations comprised 9.2% of Oxford's population in 1991 and 3.3% in the county. According to the data from the 2001 census, the proportion had risen to 12.9%. Non-white populations are not much affected by the census assumptions noted above.

These populations contribute more than average to births, partly because of their more youthful age-structure and also because family size tends to be considerably higher; about double the national average in the case of Africans and two or three times higher in the case of Pakistanis and Bangladeshis. The fertility of Indians and West Indians, however, is closer to the national average. In Oxford in 2001, Pakistanis comprised the biggest single group (2%), followed by Chinese (1.8%) and Indians (1.8%). Overall, in 1999, 26% of births in Oxford were to mothers born outside the UK, with 12% to mothers born in the New Commonwealth, little different from the 26% and 10% respectively in 1971. (This is not the same as mothers of ethnic minority origin. It does not include births to mothers who were themselves born in the UK, but also includes mothers born in Ireland and other Western countries.) The comparable figures for the county as a whole (including Oxford) were 13% of births to mothers born outside the UK and 5% to mothers born in the New Commonwealth.

The favourable view of immigration taken by the present Government, the relaxation of work permit and marriage restrictions and the Government's dispersal policy of asylum seekers are likely to increase further the number and diversity of the foreign population in Oxford. This will, perhaps, be the most dramatic and visible change in Oxford's population in the future, making it, for a while at least, more distinct from its county than today.

Migration from overseas

Most foreign immigrants to the UK settle in London and the south-east of the country. Oxford can expect to take its share of this increased inflow, which can be expected to settle more in the city than the surrounding countryside, at least to begin with.

Projections of future immigration levels are particularly difficult. However, at the national level, the assumption in the most recent (2000-based) national population projections is for a net inflow of 135,000 per year each year for the duration of the projection (to 2051). A Home Office study in 2001, more in line with actual figures, projected increasing migration reaching 180,000 in about 2010. The actual figure of the three years (1998-2000) has been a net immigration of 180,000 persons each year, the highest level ever recorded. In the year 2000, this net overall movement comprised a net inflow of 230,000 foreign citizens and net outflow of 47,000 British citizens. No special projections exist of the migration contribution to Oxford and its county and it is difficult to know on what rational basis they could be made. The short-term projections which have been made, by the county council and Department of the Environment, Transport and the Regions (DETR), appear to assume a migration share pro rata with the rest of the country. However, the international migration estimates have been crudely truncated to make them fit the results of the 2001 census. In this extraordinary Procrustean exercise, 76,000 additional UK citizens are deemed to have left the UK every year since 1991. Accordingly, the new net migration estimates for 2000 are now 100,000 and for 2001, 126,000.

Oxford's attractions to in-migrants

Oxford's tourist industry has prompted substantial business growth (as well as gross congestion in the city centre). The globalisation of English has hugely increased demand for English teaching and admission to the universities, and the numerous language and correspondence schools. The Oxford name makes convenient advertising copy. As well as the growth of employees, language and other schools further swell the transient population of students, now estimated to be up to 30,000 at peak times of year. Quite apart from student numbers, Oxford's academic activities have succeeded in attracting a number of major new scientific and bio-medical research centres, all of which bring new employees into the Oxford region, although less so into the city itself. There, house prices, stoked by population growth, are becoming prohibitive and may have a self-corrective deterrent effect on further in-migration.

'Push' as well as 'pull' factors influence movement to Oxford. While London remains highly attractive to overseas migrants and to younger people from all parts of the country, its increasingly diverse composition, its congestion and crime prompt others to move out. The poor performance of schools in some boroughs, with their language and other problems, contribute particularly to the outflow of families with school age children. By contrast, Oxford's state and especially private schools enjoy a high reputation, which for some in-migrants determine the details of their location in Oxford. Educational considerations, the attractions of suburbs and the motorway link have made North Oxford, as well as many of the rural villages, particularly attractive to richer newcomers. On a small scale, for example in parts of inner North Oxford, their demand for substantial accommodation near schools has reversed a previous trend for larger houses to fall into multiple occupation or institutional use and provoked, with other factors, a rise in house prices to make the £1 million house commonplace in some areas. Despite these attractions, migration to Oxfordshire from other parts of the UK has been relatively modest, thanks partly to planning controls. Since 1950, net in-migration has been about 3 per 1000 of population per year.

Projections of the future population of Oxford and Oxfordshire

Projection of future local population is particularly difficult. Future growth and composition at local level, as we have seen, depend much more on migration in and out than on the natural processes of birth and death, and migration is much more difficult to forecast. This is partly because of the diverse processes of migration and its uncertain duration and potential repetition by the same individual. This is compounded by the frailty of data relating to it. Britain, unlike most continental countries has no population register and no routine way of knowing where people are living or where they have come from. In most European countries, new residents must register locally and are not entitled to local services until they do. Migration levels are estimated from changes in NHS registration, responses to surveys and questions in the decennial census on residence in the previous year and other partial, obsolete or fallible sources. Local authorities have rating lists and electoral rolls and know where planning permission has been given for new dwellings or other uses. So, while something can be said about migration, serious health warnings about data must be kept in mind.

Oxford – growing in a straight jacket?

Partly for these reasons, projections even for regions are only made for a limited period into the future and for local areas on an even shorter time-scale. As far as they go (to 2021) the official 1996-based projections for Oxfordshire show considerable growth from 628,000 in 2001 to 694,000 in 2021 – an increase of 67,000 or 11%. The city was then projected to increase from 141,000 to 150,000 by 2021 – a 6.5% increase.

Population growth in the South East in general, and for Oxfordshire and Oxford in particular, runs headlong into several obstacles, some of them deliberate. Although most of the economic growth in the country has been in the southern part of England, the population of the South East as a whole has not greatly increased in response until recently. One of the reasons for this modest growth in Oxfordshire as elsewhere in the region is the severity of the planning process. The councils in most counties in the South East, notably the more attractive coastal ones, consider themselves to be full and their policies strongly oppose anything other than the minimal increase in new dwellings proposed for them. In Oxfordshire, the plan is to concentrate new growth in just four areas: Banbury, Bicester, Didcot and Witney, with results familiar to any traveller.

The city is itself hemmed in by planning constraints and its green belt in which development is supposedly forbidden. This barrier to development, the second in the country after London's, was set up in 1956, its inner boundary coinciding roughly with the ring road of 1965, though the detailed line was not confirmed until 1992. There have been many breaches, almost all by the council itself, most notably with the Greater Leys estate, built to accommodate central Oxford residents evicted from residential areas demolished for retail and parking, notoriously St Ebbe's. These apart, room for expansion of resident population in the city is seriously limited by the shortage of building land, which only occasionally becomes free from other uses.

The expansion of new private housing in the canal side sites in North Oxford taken out of industrial use in the 1990s is an unusual exception. There will be more of this, but not much – Oxford has little of the derelict or brown land on to which development is meant to be focussed in current policies. Instead, further pressure for more dwellings is likely to lead to more town cramming as the gardens of old, larger houses are built over at higher density and green spaces disappear. Infill development in the spaces between the Victorian houses is a further threat to the city's heritage. The pressure to encroach on the green spaces within Oxford's boundaries will be familiar to most readers. In June 2002 it was announced that the city council intended to make further breaks in the green belt for new housing estates.

Household growth and housing demand

Changes in population are quite different to changes in the number of households and therefore changes in the number of dwellings required to accommodate the people. One of the striking changes in 20th century Western society, very clear throughout Britain, has been the decline in the size of households. In 1901, the average household in Britain had 4.7 members, very much the same number as in previous centuries. As before, the core of that household was the nuclear family. Now average household size is down to 2.4 persons per household and a quarter of all households comprise just one person. Much of this decline is due to the reduction of family size to a two child family or less. Single person households have increased among young and old, with longer survival of widows and widowers. The national household projections of the DETR expect average household size nationally to decline further from today's 2.4 to 2.15 by 2021. Oxford is unlikely to avoid the same trend. This is how even a population which is increasing relatively slowly can exert a bigger pressure on housing by distributing itself into a growing number of smaller households.

Thus the household projections for Oxford are forecast to increase further, from 52,200 to 53,399 in 2011. In the county outside Oxford, the growth will be more marked, as population is still growing quite strongly. 23,000 new households are expected in the next ten years, a 12% increase, equivalent in terms of new dwellings to a new town almost half the size of Oxford. These household projections are related to the more modest population projections used by the county council and may just for that reason be underestimates. Indeed, the Regional Planning Guidance Note No 4 issue of Regional Planning for the South East require a further 2430 dwellings a year to 2016 (not 2011) – 12,500 more.

This forecast, and any planning related to it, may turn out to be a considerable underestimate. First, it is likely to come under pressure because household growth projections have not yet caught up with the upswing in international migration to the UK. Official projections estimate that an extra 40,000 immigrants per year would create an additional 450,000 households by 2021. Given current actual immigration and if Oxford is assumed to receive its proportional share of this increase, that would mean an additional 23,000 households by 2021. That would double the projection to 2011: almost a whole new Oxford, not half an Oxford.

Conclusions

Oxford's future population then will mirror that of the country in general and in particular that of the South East. While the rapid population growth of the two previous centuries will not be repeated, there is no prospect of an end to growth, as might have been expected twenty years ago. Despite the diminishing rate of population growth from natural increase, migration will provoke further increase, and more than that forecast in current official projections. This is partly because new proposals will weaken the power of local authorities to oppose new house building. Oxford and its county are attractive economic growth areas close to London. Unless Government changes its policy on international migration and on planning, their populations will continue to grow. The trend towards smaller households will magnify the effect of population growth on demand for housing. The boundaries of Oxford and the land-use in the growth areas of the county are likely to be transformed.

Within this growth, three sections of the population deserve special attention. The immigrant and ethnic minority population and the numbers of the elderly will increase faster than the rest of the population will increase, becoming perceptibly more numerous. The ethnic minority population will grow through the migration noted above and also through its own high level of natural increase. The elderly will increase through the inevitable process of population ageing. Official projections expect the number of persons in Oxford over age 65 to increase from 18,000 in 2001 (12.7%) to 22,000 (14.4%) in 2021 and in Oxfordshire from 87,000 (13.9%) to 126,000 (18.2%). The shape of the age structure, however, ensures that the older population will grow much faster after 2021 but detailed projections do not extend that far. All these figures are lower than the corresponding national figures, a consequence in part of the movement of younger people into Oxford. Under the present financial regime it seems that the only option for university survival is growth and both Oxford's universities are planning on future growth in numbers of up to 1% per year.

Growth in the ethnic minority population and in the student population will tend to make the city more distinct from its county than at present. Oxford will become a more crowded place, with more pressure on its green spaces and on the facilities of its centre. Some of these trends, such as that towards population ageing are unavoidable. Others are not. Destiny is not all demographic; democracy has its place, too. Policies on migration, planning, higher education and the rest can all change and change again. The surprises of the last fifty years should guard us against too much confidence about forecasting the shape of the future.

The Transport Problem - Some Solutions

By John Preston

Introduction

The aim of this chapter is to provide a vision of transport in Oxford, both in the immediate future, up to 2010, and beyond. Oxford has a history of contested transport discourses that can be dated back at least to 1769 and the construction of New Road in the castle's grounds. The most notorious dispute centred around the post war plans to build an inner relief road along Christ Church Meadow, as described in Mark Barrington-Ward's 'Overview'. Such plans were eventually replaced in 1972 by the balanced transport policy which, although it had some successes, did not eradicate traffic congestion and the associated environmental problems in the central area.

Moreover, following the deregulation of buses in 1986, a new problem emerged – that of bus congestion, most markedly on Cornmarket Street. As a result, the Oxford Transport Strategy (OTS) was developed which in June 1999 led to the closure of the High to through traffic, except buses, and the removal of buses from Cornmarket Street (see attached map p.141). This policy has itself been controversial. In particular, retail activity appeared to have declined by 10% in the first year of the new traffic scheme. Although much of this decline might have been due to external factors, retailers blamed the traffic measures. Some concessions have subsequently been made to placate the retail lobby, particularly with respect to short term parking provision, leading one observer to believe that policy has mutated from an emphasis on the environment to an emphasis on economic development.[1]

The recent past

Gaining a clear picture of what transport has been like in Oxford in the recent past is not straightforward, as data are limited.

Table 1: Vehicles Entering the Central Area in an Average 24 Hour Period (all figures rounded to the nearest thousand)

1980	1990	1995	1998/9	1999/00
54,000	60,000	59,000	54,000	43,000

Note: Transport Studies Unit (TSU) estimates based on Triesman (1999),[2] Oxfordshire County Council and City Council (2000)[3] and EMITS (2000).[4]

Table 1 shows data on the number of vehicles entering the centre of Oxford on an average weekday. This data comes from a combination of automated and manual traffic counts, rounded to the nearest 1,000. It should be treated as indicative rather than definitive. It suggests that traffic levels were broadly constant in the central area between 1980 and 1998/9, albeit with some fluctuation between 54,000 and 60,000 vehicles per day. This might be consistent with a hypothesis of a saturated road network in which traffic demand is broadly in equilibrium with the supply of road space, with variations due to changes in vehicle composition, road works, weather and seasonal fluctuations.[5] Any road space vacated, for example, by park and ride users would be taken up by previously latent demand from other motorists. The measures introduced in 1999 upset this equilibrium by withdrawing some road space from the private motorist and re-allocating it to bus users, cyclists and pedestrians. The result is an estimated 20% reduction in traffic in the central area, with a 24 hour average of 43,000 in-bound movements. This is equivalent to a 12 hour (7 am – 7 pm) flow of 34,000 vehicles. This might represent a temporary disequilibrium whilst motorists learn how to use the new road allocations. By 2001, this flow had increased to 37,000, although this still represents an approximately 15% reduction on the 1998 flows.[6] It is interesting to note that in 1949 (when petrol rationing was still in force) the 12 hour in-bound vehicle flow was recorded as 26,000.[7]

Table 2: Persons Entering the Centre of Oxford in an Average 24 Hour Period

	Cycle	Bus & Coach	HGV	LGV	Motor-Cycles	Cars & Taxis	TOTAL
1991	9,000	21,000	2,000	3,000	2,000	42,000	79,000
%	11	27	2	4	2	54	
1999/2000	8,000	31,000	1,000	3,000	1,000	27,000	71,000
%	11	44	1	4	1	39	

Note: TSU estimates based on Oxfordshire County Council and Oxford City Council (2000)[8]

Table 2 makes some estimates of person movements into the centre of Oxford by different modes of transport, based on data collated by the city and county councils. For 1999/2000, TSU has estimated that 26,000 people entered central Oxford using local buses. An additional 5,000 used park and ride, giving an estimated 31,000 using buses. From this, it is estimated that the total number of people entering the city is 71,000 per day. The city and county councils also estimate that local bus use has increased by 50% since 1991. This would suggest bus usage at 21,000 per day in 1991 and the total number entering the city as 79,000. This would in turn indicate a 10% decline in people entering the central area over a 10-year period (excluding walking and rail). This is likely to be largely due to reduced through traffic. It is estimated that pedestrian flows in the central area have increased by 8.5% between 1998 and 2000.[9]

Table 3: Vehicles Entering the Central Area 2000

	Car & Taxi	Bike	Bus & Coach	HGV/LGV	Motorbikes
24 hours	24,000	9,000	3,000	4,000	2,000
12 hours	18,000	7,000	2,000	6,000	1,000
%	55	21	7	13	4

Note: TSU estimates based Chevasse (2001)[10]

Table 3, in conjunction with Table 2, suggests that the transport system exhibits relatively low loads, with the mean number of occupants per car being 1.1 and the mean number of occupants per bus being 10. This indicates that promoting car sharing initiatives and bus use are likely to be beneficial policies.

Table 4: Vehicles Entering the Outer Cordon. 12 Hours 7 am – 7 pm

1991	1995	1998/9	1999/00
70,000	76,000	79,000	84,000

Note: TSU estimates based on EMITS (2000)[11] and Chevasse (2001)[12]

Tables 1 to **3** refer to the inner cordon; table 4 presents data with respect to an outer cordon based on the outer ring road. It suggests that between 1991 and 1998/9 traffic crossing the outer cordon increased by around 13%. Much of this might represent car-based activity displaced from the central area. In 1998, 80% of the in-bound traffic crossing the outer cordon in a 12 hour period were cars. As a result of OTS, traffic on the outer ring road has been estimated to have increased by 7%. If this increase also applies to traffic crossing the ring road, then we estimate that this leads to 84,000 vehicles crossing the outer cordon of which 67,000 are cars. The corresponding estimate for the inner cordon is 33,000 vehicles of which 18,000 are cars. This suggests that journeys into the central area are no longer the dominant car movement in Oxford.

These figures are consistent with county council estimates that between 1986 and 1996 traffic flows across the inner cordon fell by 4%, whilst traffic flows across the outer cordon increased by 12%.[13] In the rest of the county, there have been more substantial road traffic increases. Over a ten-year period, road traffic in Oxfordshire has increased by around 26%.

Table 5: Population and Car Ownership Change

	1981	1991	2001	**2011** (Estimate)
Population – Oxford ('000)	130	130	140	146*
% change		0	+8	+12
Population – Oxfordshire ('000)	541	581	623	682*
% change		+7	+15	+26
Cars per household – Oxford	0.70	0.83	0.93	1.02
% change		+18	+32	+46
Car per household –Oxfordshire	0.98	1.17	1.25	1.32
% change		+19	+28	+35

*Based on number of new homes, assuming 2.5 persons per household.
Source: Oxfordshire County Council (1999)[14]

From **Table 5**, TSU estimate that between 1991 and 2001 car ownership in Oxfordshire has grown by at least 17% (and even greater than this if we assume household growth has been greater than population growth). This suggests a strong correlation between growth in car use and growth in ownership. The M40, only completed in 1991, led to an initial 6% reduction of traffic on the rest of Oxfordshire's roads. However, it is now carrying up to 90,000 vehicles per day on the busiest stretch in the county, between Junctions 8 and 9. The A34 carries similar levels of traffic north of Oxford, whilst along the western bypass it carries around 60,000 vehicles per day. Excluding the main trunk roads (the M40, A34 and A43), the county council estimates that Oxfordshire traffic levels in 1999 were 11.19 million vehicle kilometres per day or around 18 km per inhabitant per day.[15]

Other than flow data on the principal trunk roads, there is little data available on Oxford's transport links with the rest of the country.

Table 6: Train Services Changes

Number of direct trains per weekday (one direction)			
	1982	**2000**	**% change**
London – Oxford (fast)	18	37	+106
Reading – Oxford (stopping)	24	35	+46
Oxford – Stratford-upon-Avon	0	5	new service
Oxford – Banbury (stopping)	4	10	+150
Oxford – Bicester	0	12	new service
Cross Country via Oxford	17	18	+6
Oxford - Bristol	0	13	new service
Oxford – Cotswolds – Worcester	9	15	+67

Source: Oxfordshire County Council (2001)[16]

Table 6 shows that there have been large increases in train services. There has also been a dramatic increase in the number of express coaches linking Oxford with London, Heathrow and Gatwick as well as Stansted (via Cambridge) and Luton.

The future – a 'business as usual' scenario assessment

Two documents give us an insight into what the immediate future of transport in Oxford might be like. The first is the national ten-year transport plan, Transport 2010. Although with few direct references to Oxford or Oxfordshire, this plan proposes an estimated 77% increase in real terms in transport investment focused particularly at rail and local public transport.[17] Aspirational targets are also set to reduce national car traffic growth from 22% to 17% between 2000/2001 and 2010/2011 (i.e. a 23% reduction in the growth rate). In addition, national passenger rail travel is forecast to increase from 23% to 51%, although these forecasts were made prior to the Hatfield train disaster in October 2000 and Railtrack being placed into receivership in the following year. There are also aspirations to increase national bus use by 10% and to increase walking and cycling.

These targets have been followed up at a local level through a second set of documents related to the Local Transport Plan (LTP). In Oxfordshire County Council's road traffic reduction report,[18] a target is set to reduce traffic growth in the period 2000 to 2015 to half its forecast levels – in other words a 14% growth over this period - rather than a 28% growth. More detailed targets are set for Oxford itself: firstly to reduce traffic growth at the inner Oxford cordon of radial routes by 2% per annum below the forecast growth for Oxford. The report notes that between 1991 and 1996 traffic growth for Oxford (based on DETR's TEMPRO model) was 8% but traffic across the inner cordon declined by 3% (10% less than forecast over the 5 year period – hence the 2% per annum target). In the same period, traffic growth at the outer cordon was less than 4% - hence the basis for the 1% per annum reduction. It is instructive to note that the county council estimated that between 1991 and 1996 there was a 5.9% increase in the number of households and a 4.8% increase in the number of cars per household in Oxford but that traffic grew by 8.3%, rather than the 11.0% that might be expected if the distance travelled in each car is held constant. This is again evidence that a capacity constraint is operating in Oxford.

Further aspirational targets are given in the 2001 Oxfordshire County Council's Local Transport Plan[19], which is monitored by annual progress reports. With respect to urban bus use, the county council has a target of a 5% per annum increase. A similar target is set for passenger rail throughout the county, with rail to cater for 5% of journeys to central Oxford by 2002. Table 7 suggests that rail is currently accounting for 4% of such trips. With respect to cycling there is a target to broadly double usage between 2001 and 2011 and to increase the level of walking by 10% between 2000 and 2004.

Table 7: Projection of Persons Entering the Centre of Oxford in an Average 24 Hour Period

	Cycle	Rail	Bus & Coach	HGV	LGV	Motor-Cycles	Cars & Taxis	TOTAL
1999/2000	8,000	3,000	31,000	1,000	3,000	1,000	27,000	74,000
%	11	4	42	1	4	1	36	
2009/2010	16,000	5,000	50,000	1,000	3,000	1,000	25,000	101,000
%	16	5	50	1	3	1	25	

Note: TSU estimates. From Table 5 the number of cars is estimated to increase by 14.4% over this period, but due to capacity constraints this is limited to a 10.9% increase in traffic. If the inner cordon target is to be achieved, traffic reduction of 9.1% will apply to private motorised transport.

In **Table 7** we make some estimates about the likely changes in travel to central Oxford over a ten-year period, based on the somewhat heroic assumption that the LTP and related targets are met. The caveats we outlined for earlier tables continue to apply. However, some interesting results emerge. The number of people entering the central area is forecast to increase from 74,000 (now including rail) in 1999/2000 to 101,000 in 2009/2010 (also including rail). The number of people entering the city centre is thus expected to increase by more than one-third. However, modal shares are expected to change dramatically, with public transport (bus and rail) expected to increase from a 46% to a 55% share and cycling from 11% to 16% but private motorised transport would decline from 42% to 30%. If such targets were achieved, the twin objectives of enhancing the economic vitality of the central area and of improving the environment would seem to have been realised.

How would these changes be achieved? The LTP suggests a package of measures. The OTS would continue, with fine-tuning of traffic systems to maximise effectiveness and an ongoing review of parking controls and improvements to cycle facilities. Short-term improvements would include repaving in Broad Street, Cornmarket Street and Magdalen Street, better bus passenger facilities and additional pedestrian crossings, along with better signage. In the medium term, buses would be re-directed away from Queen Street, contingent on a new bus hub as part of a redeveloped Westgate Centre. The principles of the OTS would be extended to Headington, where the concentration of health service provision is leading to serious traffic problems, particularly in relation to parking, and park and ride sites are being expanded. Transport strategies are also being developed for the surrounding towns of Abingdon, Banbury, Bicester, Didcot and Witney, although generally with a greater emphasis on highway capacity improvements and less on parking management. Eventually, Expressway Oxford might be developed to provide a high quality bus based rapid transit system linking central Oxford to the Redbridge, Peartree and Water Eaton park and ride sites and possibly beyond to Abingdon, Bicester and Witney. This might coincide with the redevelopment and relocation of Oxford railway station.

Other projects that will be pursued include changing attitudes to travel through programmes such as Better Ways to School, to be implemented in 10% of Oxfordshire's schools by 2004, and Green Travel Plans, to be implemented by 5% of employers with over 200 employees by 2005. These targets seem somewhat unambitious and perhaps should be increased as part of a wider drive towards Environmental Quality Statements.

There would also be major schemes to promote public transport. A bus lane on the A40 would dramatically improve bus times between Oxford and Witney and possibly lead to the development of long-range park and ride in Witney. Two new rail stations (at Grove and at Kidlington) would be developed on the existing rail network. A new long distance east-west rail service might be developed to link Oxford with Bedford and with Ipswich and Norwich (via Cambridge). A hierarchy of bus services would be developed, based around premium routes that serve the main centres and have high levels of bus priority and quality interchange facilities. Interlink routes would serve those areas not covered by the premium routes, but would utilise the premium routes' infrastructure as much as possible. Feeder services would serve more remote areas and link into the premium and interlink routes. Community transport would serve the most remote areas. There may well be scope for improved co-ordination of transport provided by health, social and education services, assisted by advances in information technology. Quality bus partnerships will assist in the

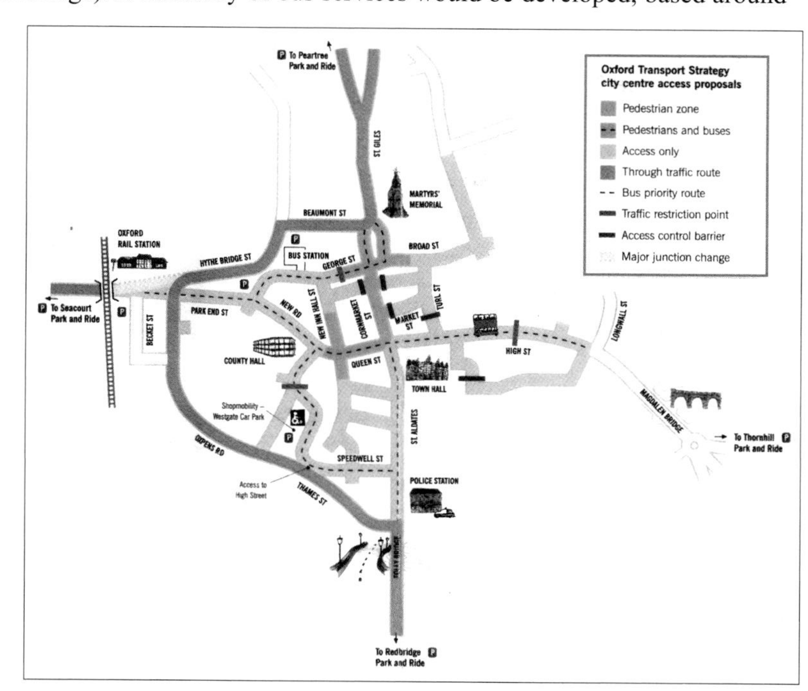

The new Water Eaton Park and Ride, Oxford.
Photo courtesy Oxfordshire County Council

development of the overall network. The achievement of truly integrated ticketing will remain problematic whilst the market is shared by two major operators and the 1998 Competition Act applies to the bus industry.

The future – alternative scenarios

On the face of it, the future for transport in Oxford appears to involve a win-win situation in which the economic vitality of the central area will be enhanced, whilst the environment will be improved by the shift to greener modes. Perhaps more priority should be given to improving the environmental performance of the bus fleet, possibly through the greater use of alternative fuels.

However, there is a more pessimistic scenario in which the use of private motorised transport to the central area does decline in the way that is envisaged but that the greener modes do not make up the shortfall. Instead, people travel by car to destinations other than central Oxford and, as a result, overall traffic growth is greater than that forecast. Particular pressure would be placed on the outer ring road, leading to the revival of capacity enhancement proposals such as the Tin Hat scheme to bypass North Oxford.[20] This may result in a lose-lose situation in which the city centre's economic vitality declines and the environment continues to be degraded by increased car traffic.

Such perverse outcomes may be limited by strict land use planning which prevents out-of-town developments. However, it could be argued that although current planning policy partially prevents out-of-town development, through maintenance of the Oxford green belt, it also encourages it through concentrating developments on the country towns beyond the green belt, particularly Banbury, Bicester, Didcot and Witney. Although these towns are designed so that population and employment are broadly balanced, you cannot ensure that people who live in a small town also work in it.[21] Further integration of transport and land use planning is needed. Arguably the current integrated transport studies for these towns only partially address this problem.

Given the above, two alternative scenarios might be postulated. The first is a more radical pro-environment policy that seeks a more substantial car (and bus) free central area in Oxford, with more extensive facilities for cyclists and pedestrians. Exemptions for environmentally friendly vehicles might be considered. This might be accompanied by an emphasis on high-density commercial and residential developments and on the promotion of car clubs to limit individual car ownership. This policy might be seen as part of a wider move to promote an urban renaissance in Oxford.[22] It would need to be supplemented by greater emphasis on traffic demand management in surrounding towns (both within the county and beyond), particularly parking controls. The second scenario would be a counterpoint to the first, being a broadly pro-car policy. This would involve relaxing parking restrictions and charges in Oxford and providing some new road infrastructure that would incorporate the best practices of the environmental management of highways. However, neither option seems realistic, reviving the contested discourses surrounding the OTS and a relief road for the High respectively.

Conclusions

So what of the future? Given the continued questioning of OTS, it is understandable that the county council will proceed cautiously, despite the ambitious targets it has set itself. It is likely that where policies are implemented, a finer attention to detail will be paid. We should expect new policies to be implemented slowly, particularly where there is no ready consensus, and should not be surprised if targets are not met.

However, there does seem to be some consensus that the strategy is broadly correct. Most participants in the transport policy debate subscribe to an economically vibrant city centre and an improved urban environment. The arguments are largely about the pace of change and of detailed implementation issues. Perhaps we should not expect, or demand, excessive change over the next ten years which might be seen as a period of consolidation for existing policies. However, in the ten years after that it may be time to be more radical and in particular consider the utilisation of policy instruments that have so far been neglected in the Oxford transport discourse – road user charging and workplace parking levies.

Such tools could deliver traffic reductions throughout the road network if designed to do so and would provide an incentive for modal shift. They could, following the 2000 Transport Act, also provide an earmarked revenue stream for public transport (eg Expressway Oxford) and other enhancements, hence overcoming an important financial constraint. However, it is likely that such policies will also attract public opposition. We may well need a further ten years of congestion and environmental degradation before attitudes shift sufficiently to support such measures.

In short, there is no utopian vision for transport in Oxford in the twenty-first century. Progress is more likely to be made by consistent policy evolution, at the local, county, regional and national levels, rather than by technological, or indeed policy, revolution. The policy emphasis will need to switch from the central area of Oxford to the rest of the city and county, thus meeting a long-standing criticism.[23]

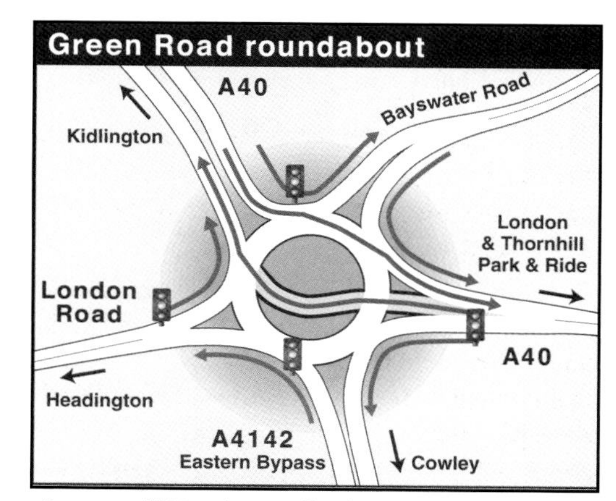

Proposed "Hamburger" solution for Green Road Roundabout.

© Courtesy Oxford Mail

References

1. Dudley, G. (2002) "Integrated Transport and Idea Mutation: Flexible Policy Communities and the Case of the Oxford Transport Strategy". Mimeo, Centre for European Politics, Economics and Society, University of Oxford.
2. Triesman, M. (1999) "How the County Preserves the Green Belt". Oxford Magazine, 8th week, Hilary Term, 2-9.

3. Oxfordshire County Council and Oxford City Council (2000) "Oxford Transport Strategy. Assessment of Impacts. November 2000".

4. Environmental Monitoring of Integrated Transport Strategies (EMITS) (2000) Third Annual Report. 1998/9. (See also: www.oxfordshire.gov.uk/emits/)

5. Mogridge, M. (1990) "Travel in Towns. Jam Yesterday, Jam Today, Jam Tomorrow". Macmillan, Basingstoke.

6. Oxfordshire County Council (2002) Local Transport Plan. Annual Progress Report 2002

7. Gullick, C.F.M.R. (1954) "Communications". In Martin, A.F. and Steel, R.W. (Eds.) "*The Oxford Region. A Scientific and Historical Survey*". Oxford University Press, Oxford.

8. Oxfordshire County Council and Oxford City Council (2000) op. cit.

9. Oxfordshire County Council (2000) "*Road Traffic Reduction Report – 2000.*"

10. Chevasse, R. (2001) "*Cycling in Oxford. Creating a Viable Alternative to Car Based Transport Systems*". Dissertation, School of Geography and the Environment, University of Oxford.

11. EMITS op. cit.

12. Chevasse, op. cit.

13. Oxfordshire County Council (1999) "*Transport in Oxford.*"

14. Ibid.

15. Oxfordshire County Council (2000) op. cit.

16. Oxfordshire County Council (2001) "*Oxfordshire Local Transport Plan 2001-2006*".

17. Preston, J. (2000) "*The Economics of Transport Investment.*" Transport Studies Unit, Ref. 902, University of Oxford.

18. Oxfordshire County Council (2000) op. cit.

19. Oxfordshire County Council (2001) op. cit.

20. Scargill, D.I. and Scargill, K.E. (1994). "*Containing the City: The Role of Oxford's Green Belt*". School of Geography Research Paper, University of Oxford.

21. Headicar P. and Curtis, C. (1998) "*The Location of New Residential Developments: Its Influence on Car Based Travel*". In Banister, D. (Ed.) "*Transport Policy and the Environment*" E & FN Spon, London.

22. Rogers, R.G. (1999) "T*owards an Urban Renaissance: Final Report of the Urban Task Force*". E and F.N.Spon, London.

23. Jones, P.M. (1990) "*Oxford: An Evolving Transport Policy*". Built Environment, 15, 314, 231-243.

24. Oxfordshire County Council (2001) op. cit.

Vision of an Exciting City

By Edwin Townsend-Coles

This is a book of ideas; how some citizens see improvements which could be made to what is already a city of great international renown to make it even better. In short to make it an exciting place in which to live and work and visit.

A city has to meet the needs of many different age and interest groups. It has to work well for those who find employment in it. It has to be a flourishing community. In the case of Oxford it has to be a suitable place in which to study, since the universities are the biggest employers. It has to cater for the aged and others with handicaps. It must be exciting for the young and provide for those with many diverse tastes and interests. It must also be a place which is a delight to visit: people come to Oxford from the shires and further afield in Britain and also from all quarters of the globe. How can Oxford be a place which holds the interest of so many?

The chapters in this book offer many approaches to this question. There are some disagreements. That is not surprising. Each chapter represents the individual interests and ideas of the writer. The volume is held together by the desire of all to improve the city. Many of the contributions deal with issues of policy. This final chapter makes no apology for highlighting some of the details. It is important to settle policies with grand brush strokes. Unless equal care is given to details, fine ideas can so easily fail to achieve the desired aims.

It has to be recognised that Oxford is not an easy place in which to have visions of a better place. Founded around a major crossroads in the southern Midlands, it has grown into a compact city with no open lung in the centre. It has always been a magnet for traffic from all directions. Most cities have a central communal space which gives a feeling of openness and allows leisured access for pedestrians. Oxford has no such facility. The centre of the city has grown somewhat distant from its rivers - many visitors are unaware that Oxford has a river - and also from the two fine open spaces, Christ Church Meadow and the University Parks, and more remote still from Port Meadow. The one central open lung which the public could have enjoyed, the castle and prison site, has now been handed over to a developer for two centuries and part will be converted into a luxury hotel for the few. It has also to be remembered that large plots in the centre are the preserve of the old university and its colleges. Whilst this fine assemblage of buildings is what makes Oxford a magnet for visitors, it is not always beneficial especially when so much of the centre is open to visitors only at very restricted times and when so many permanently closed doors give a dead effect to a road.

In seeking to make Oxford more exciting for all, what are the primary facets to be considered? I suggest the following: it must be a clean, safe and flourishing city, have a reliable and efficient system of public transport, provide a diversity of amenities and, above all, exude a sense of being proud of itself and welcoming to all. This chapter will examine each of these and suggest what could be done over the next decade or so to make Oxford a really exciting place for all.

To be a clean, safe and flourishing city entails it being under the control of good local government. Oxford suffers from having two local authorities controlling it which can lead to unnecessary disharmony, misunderstandings and loss of efficiency. During the ensuing decade, I envisage sense at last prevailing and Oxford, somewhat expanded to include neighbouring settlements, reverting to being under the control of one unitary authority. This will result in all decisions relating to the city being taken by councillors who know and understand its needs, and on whom community pressure can be directed.

In most of the centre the roads are narrow. Extra concern needs to be taken to make them safe for all and much greater care taken to make the thoroughfares both in the centre and in the main roads leading out from it as safe as possible for pedestrians and cyclists. Oxford is a city of cyclists and greater emphasis should be placed on providing better cycle routes. Greater safety for all depends on the police force being given the resources needed. As I write, this appears to be something the Government has not grasped. When I hear much publicity being lavished on increases in the national police force by perhaps a thousand or so I realise how inadequate that is since the figures for expansion usually amount to perhaps Oxford having one extra policeman; hardly a robust response to what is needed. During the decade under review, public demands for more bobbies on the beat should move the authorities to do something about it.

The whole of the centre, that is from the War Memorial to Folly Bridge and St Peter's College to the Plain, should be seen by the planners as a treasure to be handled with care. Efforts should be made to treat each road as worthy of special consideration and much more should be made of the intriguing alleyways leading off the High, and of Broad Street, one of the finest roads in Europe. A new plan for Broad Street will require the unselfish co-operation of all those concerned. With a wholly refurbished Cornmarket, the centre will begin to look more cared for. What the road needs to give it some form and take the eye from the buildings is to be flanked by rows of elegant and chunky street lights.

Carefully designed street lighting throughout the city can provide both better illumination in dark spots and a sense of unity to a road. There should be a determined effort to promote better shopfronts throughout; the present ragbag of designs being deplorable. Floodlighting could be introduced in several locations, especially at the University Church and Carfax. It is a great improvement having the Martyrs' Memorial illuminated.

Much more should be made of the waterways. All towpaths, including that along the Oxford Canal, should be properly maintained and linked so that walkers can easily pass from one channel to another by the provision of bridges. Especially welcome would be the provision of a footbridge linking the Isis to the Cherwell. The Canal Basin should be developed as a port for barges, with river-food restaurants on the shoreline. Throughout the city centre signage should be redesigned to provide sufficient detail to allow strangers to enjoy the pleasures of the place without overloading pavements.

One gem in the centre is the Covered Market. Sadly, Market Street has been so knocked about that it now lacks cohesion and style. My vision of the centre suggests that it will be appreciated that the Market is an important feature in the city. Its exterior should be cleaned and refurbished and unsightly adjuncts removed. Internally, both the council and the traders should realise that they have a joint responsibility to maintain the look of the place if more people, especially visitors, are to be attracted to it. Efforts should be made to ensure that the stalls represent a variety of products with emphasis on genuine crafts and distinctive foods rather than just superfluous souvenirs.

These detailed proposals, and each reader will be able to think of more, will help give to Oxford a cleaner, fresher look as being a place which is proud of itself and keen that others should see this. Experience shows that once public places are kept at a high standard of cleanliness, the public responds and vandalism is reduced. Untidiness and litter breed a general lack of concern in so many.

Oxford's Covered Market
Photo Edmund Gray

As in the rest of Britain, public transport continues to suffer from years of government neglect followed by legislation which divided our railways up into a multiplicity of pieces and opened our bus transport to unrestricted competition. Whether during the next decade the government will start to heal these wounds is a matter of conjecture. What is clear is that if our public transport is ever remotely to equal what is the norm in Europe much needs to be done. Nationally, legislation concerning relief from traffic congestion should be brought in, and locally, the Oxford Transport Strategy further refined and extended.

During the next decade the railway station should be moved. This would ease bottlenecks in services and hold out the possibility that trains run on time, a first prerequisite for improved services. Legislation would enable presently competing companies to be brought together, the eventual result being that the railway would be managed in much the same way as is Deutsche Bahn, a national private company working in Germany with strong central government support. Phased out routes could be reinstated such as Oxford direct to Bristol and Oxford to Cambridge, a useful cross country route, and Grove and Kidlington stations reopened. The guided bus system could link Witney, Abingdon and Woodstock into the rail network. The new station would be the centre for public transport from which bus routes would radiate throughout the city, county and region and a frequent shuttle bus would ply between it and the city centre. All stations in the rail network would carry signs about connecting bus routes, these being changed to include calling at stations, and all stations would be equipped with lifts and escalators to make access easier for the elderly.

Another feature learned from Deutsche Bahn is that small feeder routes from main line to country stations actually make money. This thinking is contrary to the Strategic Rail Authority which is still imprisoned in the outmoded Beeching approach. Inexpensively run, with one or two-carriage trains calling at unstaffed stations and with ticket vending machines on board for safety, these lines both serve rural areas and bring passengers to the main line. The Cholsey/Wallingford line is waiting for such treatment but so too are many others on the main lines in the country. It is all a matter of thinking positively.

Oxford came off lightly compared with other places following bus deregulation. In the minds of most there are two companies plying for custom. It is not that competition per se is undesirable, it is the manner in which the companies are legally unable to work sensibly together. Legislation could change this, opening the way for timetables to be replanned so that services on joint routes are sensibly staggered and there is joint ticketing throughout, with ticket vending machines at all principal stops to obviate long waits by buses on main routes. Roadside bus stop signs should be redesigned to give prominence to the destination of services; clear tables showing the arrival times of buses should be at all stopping places. In short, there should be a major rejuvenation of the whole bus network with regular consideration of the actual routes being operated to make sure that shifts in the population are being adequately noted and catered for. Minibuses should connect with main county services at strategic stops and take public transport to the villages. Country shops should be able to sell bus tickets.

The need to replan central bus terminals should be treated with urgency, in part because the new railway station will provide space for an integrated interchange. Electronic boards would indicate departure times and points for boarding long distance coaches, as is to be found for trains at railway stations. There should be a central ticket reservation office to deal with all services. In the city there would no longer be the necessity for the Gloucester Green bus station. However, improvements should be made in Queen Street or nearby as the main meeting point for city services.

These suggestions, and many more, will only come about if there is a demand by the public that all public transport be regularly and thoroughly scrutinised by the people who use the trains and buses. Each authority should be required by law to establish a transport forum representative of local interests which would meet regularly, before a public gallery, and report to the authority who in turn would be required to take note of and respond to the recommendations being made. In this way public transport will become a central issue to be taken seriously. Most importantly, trains and buses would be planned together, both fully supportive of each other. As is so often found in Europe, the message is that all public transport must be planned as an integral whole, not as distinct limbs. In this way, the whole county will be readily accessible and car use minimised.

Finally, what are the facilities which Oxford should be able to offer? How can we bring more excitement and fun into the city?

The improvements already outlined will help. Though essentially a university city, it is also a hub for local and regional commerce and business. It has wonderful hospitals. To the public the most obvious manifestations of commerce are the shops. Here Oxford has too readily allowed its main roads to become the preserve of the large national chains thereby depriving shoppers of the small specialist shops which give added character to a place. The city council should seek to redress the balance whenever possible.

Whether city dwellers or visitors, all need food. George Street has become the haven for restaurants. To make the area more attractive, the street should be made one way and the pavement widened thus giving restaurants the possibility of spreading on to them. To maintain the right flavour, priority should be given to enterprises offering English and continental cuisine. There would be no virtue in persuading Cornmarket cafes to spread on to the pavement as that would simply give the impression that we are a nation living off American fast food. The city council should publish annually a city food guide.

Oxford is well endowed with cinemas and theatres. However, there are significant gaps which need filling. The Information Centre should be a central ticketing agency. Urgently needed is a concert hall dedicated to providing a venue for musicians, choirs and groups of all kinds. This could be incorporated into a conference centre. Much more could be made of Gloucester Green, not only as a central market place on at least three days a week. A bandstand in the middle would enable music to be performed for much of the year at midday, afternoons and evenings. More could be made of the Cowley Road, already an exciting, cosmopolitan street with an annual carnival. College concerts should be better publicised and there should be renewed efforts to encourage amateur companies to perform out of doors during spring and summer. Buskers of high standard could be encouraged to perform, indeed Oxford could become nationally known by organising a festival for them. These endeavours, maximising the benefits which Oxford has on offer, would help to create the atmosphere that it is a fun city to be in.

At Oxpens there is space to provide sporting facilities presently lacking. An Olympic size swimming pool, all-weather tennis courts and a bowling alley would add another dimension to what is needed. Great care should be taken with landscaping, preserving room for a towpath walk along the river. In the parks it would be possible to provide recreational facilities for the young. There are many playing fields owned by colleges and private schools which are underused for much of the year. Arrangements should be promoted whereby senior secondary schools could enter into partnerships with the owners of these grounds so that more children could enjoy and gain from sporting facilities often denied to them.

Oxford will be an alive place with much happening in all parts of the city. What is therefore urgently needed is a large and well staffed Information Centre. As I write, it seems that once again our planners have underestimated the value of such a place, for the premises in Broad Street will be too small for the purpose before it opens its doors. It should be the place where information about the city is readily available and accommodation can be booked, along with tickets for theatres, concerts, river events and tourist buses. It should have comfortable areas for people to look at publications at leisure and have ready access to a coffee shop. Outside there would be a sheltered place for walking groups to assemble. Staff would be bilingual speakers of most of the common European languages and Japanese and the centre would be linked to the park and ride sites, either with staffed offices or electronically, so that visitors could obtain information about accommodation and other matters before coming into the city.

I said earlier that much of the centre of the city is university or college property. These buildings are the principal magnet for bringing visitors here. It is sad that so many who come are felt to be unwelcome when they hope to have access to buildings. It is entirely understood that colleges are essentially for education and those who live in them have work to do. Nevertheless the visitors bring prosperity to the place and deserve consideration. A better system could be established whereby both parties could be accommodated. University buildings open all day should be clearly marked and other premises, mainly colleges, should open in the afternoons, but all at the same time, and carnets of entrance tickets should be available at the Information Centre.

Oxford is an exciting city. So little needs to be done to make it that much more so. It was the intention of this chapter to suggest some pointers to that end. The Mayor of Barcelona is credited with having transformed that city into a fun place to visit and live in. He is reported as having said "we can dream dreams and turn them into reality". The same can happen here if councillors, officials and the public are really determined to do so.

Oxford Civic Society started in 1969 as a protest group to stop the wholesale destruction of the city by those determined to strangle us with roads and destroy our heritage.

Since then the Society has become an accepted voice on all urban development. We still protest when necessary; our emphasis, however, is on co-operation and advice.

The Society is a citizens' organisation with members resident in all parts of the city. It is the mouthpiece for the people of Oxford on all matters concerning the urban environment.

The Society is consulted regularly by Oxford City and County Councils and provides opinions on all urban development.

The Society believes that it is only by concerted action that our city can be defended from poor planning, pollution and the mass invasion of cars.

The Society gives citizens an opportunity to play a part in protecting our heritage and in shaping the future of this great city.

Oxford Civic Society

- Works with community groups throughout the city.
- Examines and comments on building plans submitted to Oxford City Council.
- Has representatives involved with Transport, including Cycles and Pedestrians, City Centre Management, Conservation Areas, Trees and the Oxford Canal.
- Arranges a programme of talks, walks and visits which aim to widen members' knowledge and enjoyment of all aspects of life in the city.
- Publishes a Newsletter three times a year.

www.oxfordcivicsoc.org.uk